GLIMPSES OF THE UNSEEN

Navigating the Haunting Question of Ghosts

SREEKUMAR V T

PREFACE

In the realm of the unseen, where shadows dance and whispers linger, the question of ghosts has fascinated and perplexed humanity for centuries. This book, "Glimpses of the Unseen: Navigating the Haunting Question of Ghosts," is a journey into the mysterious and ethereal, a quest to unravel the enigma that shrouds the existence of ghosts.

From the dimly lit corridors of ancient castles to the modern, technology-laden ghost-hunting expeditions, this book embarks on a comprehensive exploration of the spectral. It delves into the pages of history, where the echoes of apparitions reverberate through time, and steps into the present, where scientific inquiry seeks to demystify the paranormal.

As we navigate this intriguing terrain, we will encounter personal narratives of those who claim to have glimpsed the unseen, examine the cultural tapestry woven with ghostly threads, and scrutinize the methods and tools employed by investigators in their pursuit of the supernatural. From the psychological impact of ghostly encounters to the scepticism that surrounds the field, each chapter contributes to a nuanced understanding of the haunting question of ghosts.

This book does not seek to impose belief or disbelief but rather invites readers to join in a thoughtful exploration of the uncharted territories that lie beyond our everyday perceptions. It is an invitation to consider the possibility that there might be more to our world than meets the eye and to ponder the profound implications of such revelations.

As we embark on this journey together, let us approach the subject with an open mind, acknowledging the complexity of the unseen and the rich tapestry of human experience that weaves together the known and the mysterious. "Glimpses of the Unseen" invites you to navigate the haunted landscapes of the mind and spirit, offering a compass for those who seek to understand the ethereal and elusive world of ghosts.

SREEKUMAR V T

COPYRIGHT WARNING

©2023 by SREEKUMAR V T

CONTENTS

1.INTRODUCTION

Setting the Stage for the Unseen

In the vast tapestry of human existence, certain threads remain elusive, ethereal, and mysterious. These are the threads that weave the fabric of the unseen, a realm where shadows cast by the material world intertwine with the enigmatic presence of the unknown. This book, "Glimpses of the Unseen: Navigating the Haunting Question of Ghosts," invites you to embark on a journey into this shadowy terrain, where the line between reality and the supernatural becomes blurred, and the haunting question of ghosts beckons exploration.

The Allure of the Unseen

From ancient times to the present day, the concept of the unseen has captured the human imagination. It has manifested in folklore, mythology, and religious beliefs, transcending cultural boundaries and shaping the narratives that define our understanding of the world. The unseen is the repository of our fears and aspirations, the canvas upon which we project our hopes for an existence beyond the tangible.

Ghosts, as ethereal entities believed to inhabit this unseen realm, have been a persistent part of human culture. Whether as benevolent spirits guiding the living or malevolent entities seeking to unsettle, the notion of ghosts has left an indelible mark on our collective psyche. As we delve into the pages of history, we encounter ghost stories that span continents and epochs, each narrative a testament to the enduring fascination with the spectral.

The Evolving Landscape of Ghostlore

While the roots of ghostlore run deep in our cultural history, the contemporary landscape of ghostly exploration has undergone significant transformations. The advent of technology, coupled with advancements in scientific inquiry, has given rise to a new era of paranormal investigation. Ghost hunters armed with electromagnetic field meters, infrared cameras, and audio recording devices venture into purportedly haunted locations, seeking empirical evidence of the unseen.

Yet, as the tools of investigation evolve, so too do the questions that surround the existence of ghosts. Are these apparitions the product of overactive imaginations, or do they represent something more profound and beyond our current understanding of the natural world? The intersection of science and the supernatural is a complex and often contentious arena, where sceptics and believers engage in a perpetual dance of inquiry and scepticism.

The Personal Dimension: Encounters with the Unseen

Beyond the realms of folklore and scientific investigation lies the personal dimension of ghostly encounters. Throughout history, individuals have reported experiences that defy rational explanation—apparitions in the night, voices from the beyond, and inexplicable sensations that hint at a reality beyond the tangible. In this book, we will explore first-hand accounts of those who claim to have glimpsed the unseen, examining the impact of such encounters on their lives and beliefs.

These personal narratives, often deeply rooted in emotion and subjective experience, provide a window into the complexities of the haunting question of ghosts. They challenge us to consider the nature of reality, the resilience of belief systems, and the profound implications of acknowledging a world beyond our immediate perception.

Navigating the Haunting Question

As we navigate the haunting question of ghosts, it becomes apparent that this exploration is not confined to the realms of superstition or scientific inquiry alone. It is a journey that traverses the intersections of belief and scepticism, cultural diversity, and the ever-shifting boundaries between the known and the unknown.

In the chapters that follow, we will embark on a multidimensional exploration of the unseen. We will scrutinize the history of hauntings, investigate the cultural perspectives that shape our understanding of ghosts, and delve into the psychological dimensions of fear and belief. We will accompany modern ghost hunters on their quest for evidence and confront the sceptics who challenge the very existence of the paranormal.

This book is an invitation to embrace the complexities of the haunting question of ghosts. It is an acknowledgment that the unseen, though elusive, is an integral part of the human experience. As we navigate the shadows and seek glimpses of the unseen, we may find that the answers we uncover are as diverse and multifaceted as the stories that have been told throughout the ages. Welcome to the exploration of "Glimpses of the Unseen."

2. THE HISTORY OF HAUNTINGS

Tracing Ghostly Legends Through Time

I n the grand tapestry of human history, the spectral thread of the unseen has woven itself into the fabric of cultures across the globe. From the dimly lit corridors of ancient civilizations to the bustling streets of modern metropolises, tales of ghosts and hauntings have transcended time, leaving an indelible mark on our collective consciousness. As we embark on this exploration into the history of hauntings, we find ourselves unravelling a rich tapestry of legends, beliefs, and encounters that have shaped the haunting question of ghosts.

Ancient Echoes: Ghosts in the Chronicles of Antiquity

Long before the advent of scientific inquiry and organized religions, ancient civilizations grappled with the mysteries of the unseen. Mesopotamian cultures, such as the Sumerians and Babylonians, believed in ghosts that wandered the Netherworld, while the ancient Egyptians immortalized the concept of the soul's journey through elaborate funerary rituals. In these early narratives, the departed were not merely consigned to oblivion; they continued to exist in a realm beyond the living.

Ancient Greece, with its rich tapestry of mythology, introduced the concept of shades—shadowy remnants of the deceased residing in the underworld. The haunting tales of the vengeful Furies and the ghostly apparitions that visited the living spoke to the enduring human fascination with the otherworldly.

The Romans, inheritors of Greek culture, integrated the notion of ghosts into their belief systems. The concept of the "lemures," restless spirits of the dead, found a place in Roman rituals dedicated to placating these ethereal entities. The echoes of these ancient beliefs reverberate through the corridors of time, leaving an imprint on the foundations of Western thought.

Medieval Ghostlore: The Intersection of Religion and Folk Beliefs

As the medieval era dawned, the landscape of ghostlore underwent a transformation shaped by the intertwining forces of religious dogma and folk beliefs. The Christianization of Europe brought with it a complex tapestry of beliefs concerning the afterlife, sin, and redemption. Ghosts became entwined with concepts of purgatory, where souls lingered in a state of purification before attaining salvation.

During this time, the Church's influence permeated every aspect of life, and beliefs in ghosts were both sanctioned and controlled. Ghost stories often served moralistic purposes, reinforcing religious teachings and emphasizing the consequences of sinful deeds. The ghostly visitations in medieval literature, such as the ghost of Hamlet's father in Shakespeare's play, reflected the moral dilemmas of the age.

Simultaneously, however, medieval Europe also bore witness to a rich tapestry of folk beliefs. The idea of the Wild Hunt, a spectral cavalcade led by a supernatural figure, resonated across European cultures. This spectral procession, often associated with the souls of the restless dead, embodied the liminal space between the earthly and the supernatural.

The Renaissance and the Emergence of the Paranormal

The Renaissance marked a period of renewed interest in the classical works of antiquity, and with it, a revival of interest in the unseen. As intellectual curiosity blossomed, so did a fascination with the occult, alchemy, and the mysteries of the supernatural. The advent of the printing press facilitated the dissemination of knowledge, including treatises on ghosts and the paranormal.

During this time, figures like John Dee, a mathematician, astronomer, and advisor to Queen Elizabeth I, dabbled in the esoteric arts. The lines between science, philosophy, and the occult were often blurred, and the study of the unseen became a pursuit embraced by scholars and mystics alike.

One cannot discuss the Renaissance without acknowledging the impact of Shakespeare's works, where ghosts played prominent roles, embodying the unresolved conflicts and unfulfilled desires of the departed. The ghost in "Macbeth," for instance, serves as both a harbinger of doom and a manifestation of guilt—a psychological spectre haunting the protagonist.

The Enlightenment and the Rationalization of Ghosts

With the Enlightenment came a shift in intellectual paradigms. Reason and scientific inquiry took centre stage, challenging traditional beliefs in the supernatural. The rationalization of the world led to a more sceptical view of ghosts, with many intellectuals dismissing paranormal phenomena as products of superstition or the imagination.

However, even in the face of burgeoning scientific thought, ghost stories persisted. Gothic literature, a prominent literary genre of the 18th century, often featured supernatural elements. Writers like Horace Walpole and Edgar Allan Poe wove tales of haunted castles and spectral visitations, channelling the collective unease of a society caught between the certainties of reason and the allure of the mysterious.

Spiritualism and the 19th-century Resurgence of Ghostly Phenomena

The 19th century witnessed a resurgence of interest in the supernatural, particularly through the rise of Spiritualism. Emerging in the United States and later spreading to Europe, Spiritualism sought to establish communication with the spirit world. Mediums claimed to channel the voices of the departed, and séances became a popular form of entertainment and spiritual exploration.

The Victorian era, marked by a fascination with death and mourning rituals, saw an explosion of ghost stories in literature. Authors like Charles Dickens and M.R. James explored themes of the supernatural, reflecting a society grappling with rapid industrialization, scientific progress, and the uncertainties of the modern age.

The 20th Century: Ghosts in Popular Culture

The 20th century witnessed an unprecedented explosion of interest in ghosts, fuelled in part by advancements in technology and the mass media. Radio, television, and film became powerful mediums for transmitting ghost stories to a global audience. From classic films like "The Haunting" and "The Sixth Sense" to television shows like "The Twilight Zone" and "Ghost Hunters," the portrayal of ghosts in popular culture evolved, reflecting changing societal attitudes and fears.

Simultaneously, paranormal investigations became more sophisticated. Organizations dedicated to the scientific study of the paranormal emerged, employing tools such as electromagnetic field meters and infrared cameras to document and analyze purported ghostly phenomena. The intersection of science and the supernatural became a focal point of exploration, with researchers seeking empirical evidence of the unseen.

Contemporary Perspectives: Ghosts in the Digital Age

As we navigate the 21st century, the haunting question of ghosts persists in the public imagination. The internet has become a repository for countless ghost stories, with forums, blogs, and social media platforms providing individuals with a platform to share their paranormal experiences. The democratization of storytelling has led to a diverse tapestry of narratives, ranging from traditional ghost stories to accounts of digital hauntings.

Advancements in augmented reality and virtual reality have also opened new frontiers for experiencing the supernatural. Virtual ghost hunts and paranormal investigations allow individuals to explore haunted locations from the comfort of their homes, blurring the lines between the physical and the digital realms.

Conclusion: An Ongoing Exploration

The history of hauntings is a narrative woven into the very fabric of human experience. From the ancient civilizations of Mesopotamia to the digital age of the 21st century, the haunting question of ghosts has persisted, shape-shifting across cultures, belief systems, and technological landscapes.

As we delve into the rich tapestry of ghostlore, we find that the stories of the unseen are not merely relics of the past but living narratives that continue to evolve. Each era adds its own layer to the collective understanding of the supernatural, reflecting the hopes, fears, and uncertainties of the times.

This exploration is not a quest for definitive answers but an acknowledgment of the complexity inherent in the history of hauntings. As we navigate the twists and turns of these spectral narratives, we invite you to join us in unravelling the mysteries that have echoed through the corridors of time. Welcome to the journey into the history of hauntings, a journey that sets the stage for the glimpses of the unseen awaiting us in the chapters to come.

3.BEYOND THE PHYSICAL

Exploring the Nature of the Unseen

I n the labyrinth of human perception, where the tangible meets the intangible, lies the realm of the unseen. It is a dimension beyond the physical, where the boundaries of our senses blur, and the mysteries of existence take on ethereal forms. As we embark on this exploration into the nature of the unseen, we peel back the layers of reality to unveil a landscape where the haunting question of ghosts beckons us into the enigmatic depths.

The Veil Between Worlds

The concept of the unseen suggests a duality—an existence beyond the immediate grasp of our senses, separated by an ephemeral veil. This veil, though intangible, serves as a symbolic boundary between the tangible world we navigate daily and the unseen realm that eludes our empirical understanding. It is within this liminal space that the possibility of glimpsing into the ethereal becomes tantalizing.

Ancient belief systems often depicted this veil in various ways. In Celtic folklore, it was symbolized by thin places, locations where the boundary between the earthly and the spiritual was believed to be particularly permeable. Similarly, in Eastern philosophies, the idea of maya in Hinduism or the concept of the "between" in Tibetan Buddhism acknowledges the illusory nature of the physical world, suggesting that reality is more fluid than our senses perceive.

The Quantum Enigma: Science and the Unseen

As we navigate the complexities of the unseen, the realm of quantum physics emerges as a fascinating intersection between scientific inquiry and the mystical. Quantum mechanics challenges our classical understanding of reality, revealing a world where particles can exist in multiple states simultaneously, and the act of observation itself alters the nature of what is observed.

In the world of quantum entanglement, particles become mysteriously connected across vast distances, defying the limitations of space and time. The implications of these phenomena extend beyond the confines of the physical, hinting at a reality that transcends the boundaries of our classical understanding. While the link between quantum mechanics and the unseen remains speculative, the parallels are striking, inviting us to consider a more interconnected and dynamic universe.

Consciousness and the Unseen

At the heart of the exploration into the nature of the unseen lies the question of consciousness. Is the unseen a product of external phenomena, or does it spring from the depths of our own awareness? The intersection of neuroscience and metaphysics invites us to delve into the profound mystery of the mind and its role in shaping our perception of reality.

In theories of pan psychism, consciousness is not confined to the human mind but is considered a fundamental aspect of the universe. This perspective posits that consciousness is present at all levels of existence, from the smallest subatomic particles to the vast expanses of the cosmos. If consciousness is indeed a fundamental aspect of reality, it opens the door to the possibility that the unseen is not merely an external force but a manifestation of the inherent consciousness woven into the fabric of existence.

Ephemeral Energies and Auras

As we explore the nature of the unseen, the concept of energy fields and auras becomes a focal point of inquiry. Various cultural and spiritual traditions posit the existence of subtle energies that envelop living beings and extend into the surrounding environment. While these notions have often been relegated to the realms of metaphysics, there is a growing interest in exploring the scientific underpinnings of these ideas.

Bioelectromagnetic fields generated by living organisms, including humans, are measurable and extend beyond the physical body. These fields are a product of the electrical activity within our cells and nervous systems. While science has made strides in understanding these biofields, the connection between these energies and broader metaphysical concepts, such as auras or spiritual energy, remains an area of ongoing exploration.

The Unseen in Cultural and Spiritual Traditions

Across diverse cultures and spiritual traditions, the concept of the unseen takes on myriad forms. In Hinduism, the subtle body, composed of layers like the koshas, extends beyond the physical form, representing the interconnectedness of the individual with the universe. Similarly, the Chinese tradition speaks of qi, the vital life force that flows through all living things, influencing health and well-being.

In Native American spirituality, the unseen is intertwined with the spiritual realms inhabited by ancestral spirits and totemic entities. The shamanic practices of indigenous cultures often involve traversing the unseen realms to gain insights, healing, and guidance. These cultural perspectives emphasize a holistic understanding of reality, acknowledging the unseen as an integral part of the human experience.

Anomalies and Dimensions Beyond

The exploration into the nature of the unseen is also marked by encounters with anomalies that defy conventional explanation. Reports of apparitions, poltergeists, and anomalous phenomena challenge our understanding of the physical world. While sceptics may attribute these experiences to psychological or environmental factors, the persistence of such accounts across cultures and time periods suggests a more complex and elusive reality.

Theories involving alternate dimensions or parallel universes propose that the unseen may exist in spaces beyond our immediate perception.

If these dimensions intersect with our own, they could offer an explanation for the mysterious occurrences that transcend the laws of classical physics. The prospect of doorways between dimensions raises intriguing questions about the nature of reality and the potential for entities or phenomena to traverse the boundaries between worlds.

Psychical Research: Bridging Science and the Unseen

The intersection of science and the unseen finds a home in the field of psychical research, where scholars seek to apply scientific methodologies to the study of paranormal phenomena. Organizations such as the Society for Psychical Research (SPR) have been at the forefront of investigating apparitions, telepathy, and other phenomena that challenge conventional scientific paradigms.

While the scientific community at large remains cautious about delving into the paranormal, a dedicated group of researchers continues to explore the boundaries of human experience. The study of near-death experiences, telepathy, and the potential survival of consciousness beyond bodily death represents a frontier where the unseen and the scientific converge, offering glimpses into the mysteries that lie beyond the physical.

Exploring the Unseen Through Meditation and Altered States

The journey into the unseen is not solely an external exploration; it is also an inward odyssey into the depths of consciousness. Practices such as meditation, lucid dreaming, and the use of entheogens offer pathways to altered states of awareness where the boundaries between the self and the unseen become fluid.

Mystical traditions across the globe have long employed meditation as a means of transcending the limitations of the physical world. The expansion of consciousness through contemplative practices allows individuals to explore realms beyond the ordinary, providing insights, visions, and encounters with the numinous.

Conclusion: Navigating the Enigma of the Unseen

As we navigate the terrain of the unseen, we find ourselves in a realm where the tangible and the intangible dance in perpetual motion. The nature of the unseen defies easy categorization; it is both personal and universal, scientific and mystical, a reflection of our collective imagination and an enigma that eludes complete understanding.

The exploration into the unseen is an invitation to embrace the complexities of existence, to question the limitations of our perceptions, and to consider that reality may extend beyond the boundaries of the known. In the chapters to come, we will continue our journey, delving into the intricacies of the haunting question of ghosts and seeking glimpses of the unseen that linger on the periphery of our understanding. Welcome to the exploration of "Glimpses of the Unseen," where the nature of the unseen unfolds in a tapestry woven with threads of mystery and possibility.

4. ENCOUNTERS OF THE EERIE KIND

Personal Ghost Stories

In the vast expanse of human experience, there exists a realm where the ordinary brushes against the extraordinary, and the tangible world melds with the ethereal—the realm of personal ghost stories. These accounts, whispered in hushed tones or bravely shared, transcend the boundaries of scepticism and belief, inviting us into the intimate encounters of individuals who have glimpsed the unseen. In this chapter, "Encounters of the Eerie Kind," we traverse the shadowy corridors of personal narratives, where the haunting question of ghosts becomes more than a theoretical inquiry—it becomes an exploration of the inexplicable, the unsettling, and the mysterious.

The Looming Presence: A Childhood Encounter

For many, the first brush with the unseen occurs in the formative years of childhood—a time when the imagination is fertile ground for the extraordinary. Sarah, now a middle-aged librarian, vividly recalls her encounter with a looming presence that visited her room during the late hours of the night.

"I could feel it before I saw it," she recounts. "A heaviness in the air, like an invisible weight pressing down on me. And then, I saw it—a shadowy figure standing at the foot of my bed. It had no discernible features, just an indistinct silhouette. I couldn't move, couldn't scream. I felt both terror and fascination."

Sarah's experience is not uncommon. Many report similar encounters during childhood, raising intriguing questions about the nature of these apparitions. Are they products of an overactive imagination, or do they represent a genuine interaction with the unseen?

The Whispering Voices: An Apartment's Unseen Inhabitants

As we delve into the realm of personal ghost stories, apartments and houses emerge as theaters where the supernatural drama unfolds. Mark, a young professional living in a historic building, recounts an ongoing series of encounters with what he describes as "whispering voices."

"It started with faint whispers, almost like a distant conversation," Mark explains. "At first, I dismissed it as the sounds of neighbors. But as time went on, the whispers grew clearer, and I realized they weren't coming from outside. They were inside my apartment, yet no one else was there."

Mark's experience raises intriguing questions about the nature of residual energy or echoes from the past. Could certain locations retain imprints of past events, replaying snippets of conversations or emotions like residual energy imprinted on the environment?

The Lady in White: A Haunting Resonance

In the annals of personal ghost stories, apparitions often take on recognizable forms—a phenomenon frequently portrayed in literature and folklore. Rebecca, a teacher in her mid-thirties, shares her encounter with a spectral figure she refers to as "The Lady in White."

"I was driving home late one night when I saw her standing by the side of the road," Rebecca recalls. "She wore a flowing white dress and seemed to glow in the moonlight. As I passed, she turned and looked at me with mournful eyes. I couldn't shake the feeling that she carried a heavy sorrow."

Encounters with apparitions like "The Lady in White" prompt contemplation on the nature of these entities. Are they conscious beings with lingering emotions, or are they residual imprints, replaying moments from the past like spectral echoes?

The Haunted Object: A Family Heirloom's Secret

The unseen, it seems, is not confined to specific locations or apparitions alone. Objects, too, can become conduits for mysterious energies. James, a historian with a penchant for family heirlooms, discovered this firsthand when he inherited an antique mirror with a storied past.

"I always felt a strange energy around that mirror," James reveals. "Sometimes, I would catch glimpses of movement in its reflection—figures standing just beyond my line of sight. It was unsettling, as if the mirror held secrets of its own."

Objects carrying a sense of history or emotional weight often feature in ghost stories, inviting speculation about the potential for energies to become attached to items, weaving a haunting narrative that transcends time.

The Poltergeist Phenomenon: Unexplained Disturbances

In the spectrum of personal ghost stories, the poltergeist phenomenon stands out for its tangible and often disruptive nature. Emma, a college student living in a shared apartment, recounts a series of unexplained disturbances that left her and her roommates bewildered.

"It started with small things—objects moving on their own, strange knocking sounds," Emma recounts. "But it escalated. Furniture would be overturned when we returned home, and we would hear laughter in empty rooms. It was as if something unseen was making its presence known."

The poltergeist phenomenon challenges conventional explanations for ghostly encounters. Some attribute it to repressed psychic energy, while others question whether external forces are at play. The unsettling nature of poltergeist activity raises profound questions about the limits of our understanding of the unseen.

The Electronic Presence: Ghosts in the Digital Age

As technology advances, so too do the avenues through which the unseen makes itself known. In an era dominated by smartphones and electronic devices, reports of electronic disturbances and ghostly encounters in the digital realm have become increasingly prevalent.

Jasmine, a tech enthusiast, recounts her eerie experience with a haunted smartphone. "Apps would open on their own, and I started receiving text messages from an unknown number, each one more cryptic than the last," she shares. "It felt like the device had become a conduit for something beyond the physical."

The integration of the unseen into the digital landscape challenges traditional notions of haunting, prompting us to consider how the ethereal might interact with the electronic.

Collective Hauntings: Shared Experiences and Shared Fears

In the realm of personal ghost stories, there are instances where the unseen extends its influence beyond individual encounters. Shared experiences, whether within families, groups of friends, or communities, create a collective tapestry of haunting narratives.

The Bell Witch haunting in the early 19th century, where the Bell family in Tennessee reported poltergeist activity and encounters with a malevolent entity, stands as an example of a collective haunting. The persistence of shared experiences raises questions about the nature of belief and how the collective psyche might influence the perception of the unseen.

Exploring the Psychological Dimension: Sleep Paralysis and Haunting Hallucinations

In the exploration of personal ghost stories, the psychological dimension emerges as a critical factor. Sleep paralysis, a phenomenon where individuals temporarily experience an inability to move or speak during sleep, often accompanies vivid and unsettling hallucinations.

Benjamin, a medical student, shares his recurring episodes of sleep paralysis and the accompanying hallucinations of shadowy figures in his room. "It's as if the boundary between dreams and reality blurs," he says. "I know it's not real, but the experience is so vivid, and the presence feels so tangible."

The intersection of sleep paralysis and personal ghost stories prompts a closer examination of how the mind can conjure haunting experiences, blurring the lines between the dream world and waking reality.

Conclusion: Shadows in the Twilight Zone

As we navigate the labyrinth of personal ghost stories, the narratives shared by individuals illuminate the elusive nature of the unseen. Whether encountered in childhood bedrooms, historic buildings, or through family heirlooms, the stories resonate with a common thread—the unsettling and mysterious presence of something beyond the grasp of our understanding.

These encounters of the eerie kind prompt reflection on the nature of belief, the resilience of scepticism, and the delicate balance between the tangible and the ethereal. Are these personal ghost stories glimpses into a parallel reality, echoes from the past, or manifestations of the human psyche navigating the boundaries of perception?

In the chapters to come, we will continue our journey into the haunting question of ghosts, exploring the cultural perspectives, the scientific inquiries, and the mystical dimensions that weave together the rich tapestry of the unseen. Welcome to the exploration of "Glimpses of the Unseen," where personal ghost stories serve as lanterns guiding us through the shadows of the mysterious and the unexplained.

5. THE SCIENCE OF SPIRITS

Paranormal Investigations and Research

I n the pursuit of unravelling the mysteries of the unseen, some intrepid individuals have dedicated themselves to the scientific exploration of paranormal phenomena. Paranormal investigations and research constitute a field where empirical inquiry meets the enigmatic, where the boundaries between the known and the unknown are scrutinized. In this chapter, "The Science of Spirits," we delve into the world of paranormal research, examining the methods, challenges, and implications of applying scientific principles to the haunting question of ghosts.

The Evolution of Paranormal Investigations

Paranormal investigations have a rich history, often rooted in a quest to bridge the gap between the empirical and the supernatural. The late 19th and early 20th centuries saw the emergence of organizations like the Society for Psychical Research (SPR), which sought to apply scientific methods to the study of paranormal phenomena. Researchers within the SPR investigated mediums, documented hauntings, and explored telepathy, laying the groundwork for future generations of paranormal investigators.

As the 20th century progressed, the popularity of paranormal investigations grew, fueled in part by advancements in technology. The advent of audio and visual recording equipment provided investigators with tools to document and analyze purported paranormal activity. Today, paranormal investigations have become a global phenomenon, with countless individuals and organizations employing a range of technologies and methodologies to explore the unseen.

Methodologies in Paranormal Investigations

The scientific approach to paranormal investigations involves a careful combination of technology, observation, and analysis. Investigators often deploy a variety of tools to measure and record environmental factors, electromagnetic fields, and audio and visual phenomena. Here are some key methodologies commonly employed in paranormal investigations:

1. **Electromagnetic Field (EMF) Meters:** These devices measure changes in electromagnetic fields, as some believe that paranormal entities can manipulate these fields.
2. **Infrared Thermometers and Cameras:** Used to detect changes in temperature, as cold spots are often associated with paranormal activity.
3. **Audio Recording Devices:** Capturing electronic voice phenomena (EVP), unexplained sounds, or voices not audible to the human ear during investigations.
4. **Full-Spectrum Cameras:** Capturing images beyond the range of human vision, potentially revealing anomalies not visible under normal lighting.
5. **Motion Sensors:** Triggered by movement, these devices aim to detect the presence of unseen entities.
6. **Geiger Counters:** Measuring radiation levels, as some theories suggest that paranormal activity may be associated with changes in radiation.
7. **Historical Research:** Investigating the history of a location, including previous inhabitants, events, and tragedies, to understand potential sources of paranormal activity.
8. **Psychological Assessment:** Considering the psychological state of individuals involved, as heightened emotions or stress may influence perceptions.

These tools and methodologies are employed with the goal of capturing empirical evidence that can be analyzed and scrutinized.

While the scientific community at large often remains sceptical of paranormal investigations, dedicated researchers continue to refine their methods and seek credible evidence of the unseen.

Challenges in Paranormal Research

Paranormal research faces significant challenges, both in terms of methodological rigor and the broader acceptance of its findings. Some of the key challenges include:

1. **Subjectivity:** Paranormal experiences are inherently subjective, relying on personal perceptions and interpretations. This subjectivity poses challenges in establishing consistent and replicable research outcomes.
2. **Lack of Standardization:** The field lacks standardized protocols and methodologies, leading to variations in how investigations are conducted. This lack of standardization hinders the comparability of findings across different studies.
3. **Technology Limitations:** While advancements in technology have enhanced the capabilities of paranormal investigators, the reliability and validity of certain tools remain questionable. Critics argue that some devices may be prone to false positives or misinterpretation.
4. **Interdisciplinary Scepticism:** The interdisciplinary nature of paranormal research, spanning psychology, physics, and metaphysics, often leads to scepticism from specialists in these fields. Bridging the gap between the scientific and the paranormal remains a persistent challenge.
5. **Public Perception and Stigma:** The popular portrayal of paranormal investigations in the media, often sensationalized for entertainment purposes, contributes to scepticism and stigma surrounding the field. This makes it challenging for serious researchers to gain credibility.

Despite these challenges, dedicated paranormal researchers continue to refine their methodologies, collaborate with other scientific disciplines, and engage in ongoing discussions about how to elevate the standards of their field.

The Role of Scepticism in Paranormal Research

Scepticism is a fundamental aspect of scientific inquiry, serving as a critical lens through which researchers scrutinize evidence and hypotheses. In the realm of paranormal investigations, sceptics play a valuable role in promoting rigorous methodology and challenging unsubstantiated claims.

Organizations like the Committee for Sceptical Inquiry (CSI) advocate for scientific scepticism and have been vocal critics of paranormal claims lacking empirical support. Sceptics emphasize the importance of controlled experiments, statistical analysis, and a cautious approach to interpreting anomalous findings.

While healthy scepticism is essential for maintaining scientific integrity, it is equally important to distinguish between constructive scepticism and dismissive cynicism. Open dialogue between sceptics and paranormal researchers can foster a more nuanced understanding of the challenges inherent in exploring the unseen.

The Implications of Paranormal Discoveries

If paranormal researchers were to uncover conclusive evidence of ghosts or other supernatural phenomena, the implications would reverberate across scientific, philosophical, and cultural landscapes. Such discoveries could challenge fundamental assumptions about the nature of reality, consciousness, and the afterlife.

1. **Reevaluating Reality:** Conclusive evidence of the paranormal would necessitate a reevaluation of our understanding of reality. It could prompt a paradigm shift in scientific frameworks, challenging materialist philosophies that exclude the possibility of non-physical entities.
2. **Exploring Consciousness:** If the unseen is validated, questions about the nature of consciousness would come to the forefront. Are paranormal entities conscious beings, and what does their existence imply about the nature of consciousness itself?
3. **Ethical Considerations:** The discovery of paranormal phenomena would raise ethical considerations regarding the

treatment and interaction with entities beyond the physical realm. How should society approach communication or engagement with the unseen?

4. **Cultural and Religious Impact:** Paranormal discoveries could have profound implications for cultural and religious beliefs. It might reshape our understanding of the afterlife, spiritual realms, and the interconnectedness of life and death.

5. **Technological Innovation:** The development of technologies aimed at detecting and interacting with the unseen could open new frontiers in science and engineering. Ethical considerations would need to accompany these technological advancements.

As of now, conclusive evidence of the paranormal remains elusive, and the implications mentioned are speculative. The scientific community continues to grapple with the methodological challenges inherent in paranormal research, maintaining a delicate balance between open-minded inquiry and rigorous scepticism.

Conclusion: The Ongoing Quest for Answers

The science of spirits, as explored through paranormal investigations, remains a frontier where the known and the unknown converge. As researchers employ advanced technologies, refine methodologies, and engage in interdisciplinary dialogue, the quest for answers to the haunting question of ghosts continues.

Whether fueled by personal experiences, technological advancements, or a deep curiosity about the mysteries of the unseen, paranormal investigators persist in their pursuit of empirical evidence. The tension between scepticism and belief, subjectivity and objectivity, and the tangible and the ethereal underscores the complexity of navigating the enigmatic realms explored in "Glimpses of the Unseen."

In the chapters to come, we will further explore the cultural perspectives, historical dimensions, and mystical facets of the haunting question of ghosts. The journey into the unseen unfolds, inviting us to contemplate the nature of existence and the possibilities that linger on the periphery of our understanding. Welcome to the ongoing exploration of the enigma that is "Glimpses of the Unseen."

6.CULTURAL PERSPECTIVES

Ghosts in Mythology and Folklore

In the kaleidoscope of human cultures, the specter of the unseen takes on myriad forms, weaving through the fabric of mythology and folklore. Ghosts, phantoms, and spirits have haunted the collective imagination across the ages, transcending geographical boundaries and cultural divides. In this chapter, "Cultural Perspectives: Ghosts in Mythology and Folklore," we embark on a journey to explore how different societies have conceived, feared, and revered the ethereal entities that linger on the periphery of our understanding.

Ancient Echoes: Ghosts in Mesopotamian Mythology

In the cradle of civilization, the ancient cultures of Mesopotamia gave birth to some of the earliest depictions of the supernatural. In Sumerian mythology, the afterlife was not a final destination but a complex underworld known as the "Kur," where the spirits of the deceased continued to exist. Ghosts, known as "gidim," were believed to wander the Netherworld, their existence marked by a haunting sense of incompleteness.

As civilizations evolved, so too did the complexity of their beliefs. The Babylonians, heirs to Sumerian culture, integrated the concept of ghosts into their mythological narratives. The "utukku," vengeful spirits of the deceased, were thought to bring illness and misfortune to the living. These ancient echoes laid the foundation for later cultural perspectives on the restless dead.

Greek Tragedies and Elysian Fields: Shades of the Underworld

In ancient Greece, the realm of Hades held sway over the departed souls. The shades of the deceased, known as "kēres," were believed to inhabit the gloomy realm of the Underworld. Greek mythology abounds with tales of ghosts seeking closure or revenge, reflecting the complex interplay between the living and the dead.

The concept of the Elysian Fields, a paradisiacal afterlife reserved for heroes and virtuous individuals, introduced a nuanced view of the afterlife. While some spirits lingered in the shadowy realms, others found solace in idyllic landscapes, creating a dichotomy that resonated through the annals of Western mythology.

The Shifting Sands of Egyptian Afterlife: Ba and Ka

In the grand tapestry of ancient Egypt, the journey to the afterlife was guided by intricate beliefs surrounding the soul. The Egyptians conceived of the soul as comprising multiple elements, including the "ba" and the "ka." The ba, often depicted as a bird, represented the personality and individuality of the deceased. The ka, an individual's life force, needed sustenance even in the afterlife.

Egyptian mythology featured benevolent spirits known as "akhu," revered ancestors who could provide guidance and blessings. However, the malevolent spirits, often associated with chaos and disorder, posed a threat to the living. The intricate rituals and funerary practices of ancient Egypt reflected a cultural preoccupation with ensuring a harmonious transition to the afterlife and averting the wrath of malevolent spirits.

Norse Shades and Valkyries: Ghosts in Northern Realms

In the frigid landscapes of the North, Norse mythology painted a vivid tapestry of the afterlife. The Vikings believed in an otherworldly realm known as Valhalla, a warrior's paradise where those who died in battle were ushered by the valkyries. Yet, not all spirits found solace in such an esteemed afterlife.

The shades of the departed, known as "draugar," were believed to linger in the mortal realm, often animated by a desire for vengeance or unfulfilled obligations. These malevolent spirits, with their supernatural strength and cunning, embodied the complex relationship between the living and the dead in Norse mythology.

Yūrei and Yokai: Ghosts in Japanese Folklore

In the Land of the Rising Sun, Japanese folklore teems with spectral entities, each bearing its own cultural significance. Yūrei, often depicted as vengeful spirits with disheveled hair and white burial kimono, are believed to be souls unable to find peace due to unresolved grievances. The cultural phenomenon of "obon," a Buddhist festival honoring ancestors, reflects the profound influence of these beliefs on Japanese society.

Beyond yūrei, Japanese folklore introduces a diverse array of supernatural beings, collectively known as "yokai." Some, like the mischievous kappa or the enigmatic tengu, straddle the line between the natural and supernatural realms. Others, such as the "ubume," represent the spectral aspects of motherhood, emphasizing the cultural nuances embedded in the perception of ghosts.

Ancestor Veneration: Ghosts in Chinese Culture

In the vast tapestry of Chinese mythology and folklore, the concept of ancestor veneration takes centre stage. The living maintain a deep connection with their forebears, believing that the spirits of ancestors continue to influence the course of family affairs. The "Hungry Ghost Festival" is a poignant example of these beliefs, as families offer food and incense to appease and honor the spirits of the departed.

Chinese folklore also introduces the concept of "gui," spirits or ghosts that may have met untimely or unjust deaths. These restless entities, believed to harbor grievances, occupy a liminal space between the worlds of the living and the dead, emphasizing the cultural importance of addressing and pacifying unsettled spirits.

Medieval Europe: The Dance of the Macabre

In medieval Europe, the Black Death cast a grim shadow over the continent, reshaping cultural perspectives on death and the afterlife. The "Dance of Death" or "Danse Macabre" emerged as a recurring motif in art and literature, depicting skeletons leading people from all walks of life in a macabre dance. This artistic expression underscored the inevitability of death and the egalitarian nature of mortality.

The Christian framework also played a pivotal role in shaping cultural perspectives on ghosts in medieval Europe. The concept of purgatory, a temporary state of purification, introduced the notion of spirits lingering between heaven and hell. Penance, prayers, and rituals aimed at expediting the ascent of souls to heaven reflected a fusion of Christian doctrine and cultural beliefs regarding the fate of the departed.

The Ghosts of Southeast Asia: Spirits in Every Element

The diverse cultures of Southeast Asia are rich with beliefs in spirits inhabiting natural elements. From the Philippines to Indonesia, spirits known as "aswang," "pontianak," or "kuntilanak" are woven into the fabric of local folklore. These spirits, often associated with specific locations or natural features, exemplify the profound connection between the spiritual and the earthly.

In Indonesian folklore, the "pocong" is a ghostly figure wrapped in burial shrouds, believed to represent the soul of the deceased. The "djinn" of Islamic mythology, present across various cultures in the region, embodies the multifaceted nature of spirits, ranging from benevolent protectors to mischievous tricksters.

Dia de los Muertos: Celebrating the Departed in Mexico

In Mexico, the Day of the Dead, or "Dia de los Muertos," stands as a vibrant celebration of life and death. Far from fearing the spirits of the departed, this cultural festival invites families to honor and remember their loved ones. Altars adorned with marigolds, candles, and the favorite foods of the deceased create a colorful tapestry of remembrance.

The Mexican perspective on ghosts contrasts with some Western notions of fear and malevolence associated with the spectral realm. Instead, Dia de los Muertos reflects a harmonious relationship with the departed, emphasizing the cyclical nature of life and death.

Ghosts in Contemporary Culture: From Horror to Healing

As we navigate the 21st century, cultural perspectives on ghosts have evolved alongside technological advancements and global connectivity. The genre of supernatural horror continues to captivate audiences worldwide, with ghosts serving as iconic symbols of fear and the unknown. Yet, contemporary culture also witnesses a shift toward more nuanced portrayals of the spectral realm.

Television shows and films explore the human experience of loss, grief, and the quest for closure, providing a platform for narratives that transcend the traditional horror tropes. From "The Sixth Sense" to "The Others," storytelling has evolved to encompass the emotional and psychological dimensions of encounters with the unseen.

In some cultures, the focus has shifted from fear to healing. Practices like spirit release therapy and shamanic rituals aim to address unresolved issues between the living and the dead, fostering a sense of closure and peace. These contemporary approaches reflect an evolving understanding of the relationship between the living and the unseen.

Conclusion: Ghosts as Cultural Mirrors

The myriad cultural perspectives on ghosts serve as mirrors reflecting the values, fears, and aspirations of societies throughout history. Whether vengeful spirits seeking retribution, benevolent ancestors offering guidance, or ethereal entities inhabiting natural elements, ghosts embody the complex interplay between the tangible and the metaphysical.

As we journey through the rich tapestry of cultural beliefs, we gain insights into the human condition—our quest for meaning, our relationships with mortality, and our yearning to connect with the mysteries beyond. The haunting question of ghosts transcends mere superstition; it becomes a profound exploration of the human psyche and the enduring enigma of the unseen.

In the chapters to come, we will continue our exploration of "Glimpses of the Unseen," delving into the historical dimensions, scientific inquiries, and mystical facets that shape our understanding of the spectral realm. Welcome to the ongoing journey where cultural perspectives intertwine with the haunting question of ghosts, inviting us to contemplate the unseen threads that connect us across time and space.

7.HAUNTED LOCATIONS

Exploring Notorious Ghostly Hotspots

In the shadowy corners of the world, certain places carry a heavy veil of mystery, where the echoes of the past seem to linger, and the boundary between the living and the unseen grows thin. These are the notorious ghostly hotspots, each with its own tales of hauntings, apparitions, and inexplicable phenomena. In this chapter, "Haunted Locations," we embark on a journey to explore some of the most chilling and enigmatic places where the question of ghosts becomes more than a philosophical inquiry—it becomes a tangible reality that haunts the corridors of history.

The Tower of London: A Fortress of Phantoms

The Tower of London, standing proudly on the banks of the River Thames, is a fortress with a storied past that extends beyond its architectural grandeur. As a symbol of power and a witness to centuries of political intrigue, the Tower has earned a reputation as one of the most haunted locations in the world.

Within its stone walls, the spirits of the past are said to roam freely. The ghostly figure of Anne Boleyn, the ill-fated second wife of Henry VIII, is believed to pace the Tower's grounds, her headless apparition a chilling reminder of the tumultuous history that unfolded within these walls. Other specters include the ghostly White Lady, thought to be Arbella Stuart, and the ominous figure of the Countess of Salisbury, who met a grisly end during the Wars of the Roses.

The Tower of London's haunted reputation extends to the Beauchamp Tower, where prisoners etched poignant graffiti into the stone walls during their incarceration. As night falls, the air thickens with the weight of history, and the spectral inhabitants of the Tower continue to leave their indelible mark on those who dare to explore its haunted corridors.

Eastern State Penitentiary: Shadows of Solitude

In the heart of Philadelphia stands the imposing structure of Eastern State Penitentiary, a Gothic fortress of incarceration that once housed some of the most notorious criminals in American history. Built in the early 19th century, the penitentiary was designed to instill penitence in its inmates through solitary confinement, a method that left an indelible mark on the building's history.

The empty cells of Eastern State Penitentiary are said to resonate with the anguished whispers of former prisoners. One of the most infamous tales is that of the "Shadow Figure," a dark, indistinct form that reportedly moves through the corridors, evoking a sense of dread in those who encounter it. Visitors and paranormal investigators alike have reported eerie footsteps, disembodied laughter, and unsettling apparitions, suggesting that the imprints of suffering linger within the prison's formidable walls.

As the sun sets over the decaying cellblocks, the shadows of solitude come alive, and Eastern State Penitentiary stands as a chilling testament to the enduring mysteries of the afterlife.

The Ancient Ram Inn: England's Most Haunted Inn

Nestled in the quaint village of Wotton-under-Edge in Gloucestershire, the Ancient Ram Inn is not your typical English inn. Built in the 12th century, this charming yet ominous establishment is reputedly the most haunted inn in England, with a history steeped in occultism, tragedy, and spectral encounters.

Legend has it that the Ancient Ram Inn was constructed on the intersection of two ley lines, channels of mystical energy that some believe amplify paranormal activity. The inn's former owner, John

Humphries, claimed to have encountered a host of supernatural entities, including the spirit of a murdered girl and a demonic incubus. Guests have reported being touched by unseen hands, hearing disembodied voices, and witnessing apparitions in period clothing.

The Ancient Ram Inn stands as a portal to the otherworldly, drawing those who seek to unravel the mysteries that shroud this ancient dwelling. As night descends on the village, the inn's haunted reputation casts a spectral glow over its timeworn walls.

The Myrtles Plantation: Ghosts of the Deep South

Amidst the hauntingly beautiful landscapes of the Deep South, the Myrtles Plantation in St. Francisville, Louisiana, exudes a peculiar charm that belies its dark history. Built in 1796, this antebellum plantation is said to be home to several restless spirits, earning it a reputation as one of the most haunted locations in the southern United States.

The legend of Chloe, a former slave who met a tragic end, permeates the haunting narrative of the Myrtles. According to local lore, Chloe's spirit wanders the plantation, and her presence is sometimes captured in photographs. The grand mansion is also believed to be haunted by the spirits of other slaves and former residents, their spectral apparitions manifesting in mirrors and shadowy corners.

The Myrtles Plantation, with its grand oak-lined entrance and meticulously preserved architecture, offers a glimpse into the antebellum South. Yet, beneath the veneer of historical elegance lies a tapestry of ghostly tales, beckoning visitors to tread carefully through its rooms steeped in the echoes of bygone eras.

Aokigahara Forest: The Sea of Trees and Silent Spirits

In the shadow of Mount Fuji in Japan lies Aokigahara Forest, a place of serene beauty that harbors a haunting reputation. Also known as the Sea of Trees, this dense woodland has become synonymous with tragedy and spiritual unrest.

Aokigahara has gained notoriety as a site for suicides, with an alarming number of individuals choosing this secluded location to end their lives. The forest's eerie stillness and dense foliage create an atmosphere of isolation, amplifying the weight of sorrow that seems to permeate the air. Local legends suggest that the souls of those who have perished in the forest linger as yūrei, tormented spirits unable to find peace.

Venturing into Aokigahara is a journey into the heart of profound sadness, where the natural beauty of the forest conceals the silent struggles of those who have succumbed to its melancholic embrace. The rustling leaves and swaying branches seem to carry the whispers of the departed, creating an ethereal chorus that resonates through the Sea of Trees.

The Queen Mary: Luxury Liner Turned Ghost Ship

Once a symbol of opulence and luxury, the Queen Mary, now permanently docked in Long Beach, California, has earned a reputation as one of the most haunted ships in the world. With a history that spans the golden age of ocean liners and wartime service, the Queen Mary carries the weight of its storied past into the realm of the supernatural.

Numerous reports of ghostly encounters abound on the Queen Mary. The spirit of a young girl named Jackie, who is said to have drowned in the ship's swimming pool, is believed to linger in the area, giggling and playing pranks on unsuspecting guests. The apparitions of uniformed sailors, remnants of the ship's wartime service, have been reported throughout the vessel.

As visitors explore the elegant corridors and grand ballrooms, the Queen Mary's haunted legacy adds a layer of intrigue to the maritime glamour of yesteryear. The ship's ghostly inhabitants seem to transcend time, creating an ethereal connection between the living and those who once sailed the high seas.

Poveglia Island: Venice's Plague-Stricken Graveyard

In the lagoon of Venice, Italy, lies Poveglia Island, a place shrouded in darkness and despair. Once a quarantine station for the bubonic plague and later a psychiatric hospital, Poveglia has earned a reputation as one of the most haunted locations in Europe.

The island's soil is said to be composed in part of the ashes of plague victims, creating an eerie connection to the suffering that unfolded within its boundaries. Visitors to Poveglia report feelings of unease, disembodied cries, and sightings of ghostly figures wandering the overgrown ruins of the abandoned hospital.

Poveglia's haunted legacy extends to the chilling tales of a deranged doctor who conducted gruesome experiments on patients, adding a layer of horror to the island's tragic history. As the winds sweep through the desolate remains of Poveglia, the echoes of the plague-stricken past reverberate, and the spirits of the departed seem to linger in the mists that enshroud the island.

Waverly Hills Sanatorium: Shadows of Suffering

High atop a hill in Louisville, Kentucky, the imposing Waverly Hills Sanatorium stands as a testament to the bygone era of tuberculosis treatment and the shadowy realms of paranormal activity. Built in the early 20th century, Waverly Hills operated as a tuberculosis hospital, its grim reputation compounded by the harsh medical treatments of the time.

The sanatorium's haunting history is punctuated by tales of suffering, death, and the residual energy of those who succumbed to the ravages of tuberculosis. The "Death Tunnel," an underground passage used to transport deceased patients discreetly, is said to be a hotbed of paranormal activity, with ghostly apparitions and unexplained sounds reported by visitors and investigators.

Waverly Hills has become a magnet for paranormal enthusiasts and investigators seeking to unravel the mysteries of the afterlife. The lingering shadows of suffering that permeate the sanatorium create an atmosphere where the veil between the living and the dead appears to thin, inviting those brave enough to explore the echoes of a haunting past.

Conclusion: Portals to the Other Side

Haunted locations are more than physical spaces; they are portals to the other side, where the imprints of the past intersect with the present. Whether it's the Tower of London's historic specters, the melancholic beauty of Aokigahara Forest, or the residual energies within the Waverly Hills Sanatorium, these places embody the haunting question of ghosts.

As we traverse the corridors of these notorious ghostly hotspots, we are reminded that the unseen is not confined to the abstract realms of philosophy or folklore. It manifests in the creaking floorboards, the chilling breezes, and the inexplicable phenomena that defy rational explanation. The question of ghosts becomes a tangible exploration of the mysteries that linger in the shadows of our collective history.

In the chapters to come, we will continue our journey through "Glimpses of the Unseen," exploring the historical dimensions, cultural perspectives, and scientific inquiries that weave together the complex tapestry of the haunting question of ghosts. Welcome to the ongoing exploration of the spectral realms, where each haunted location invites us to peer into the mysteries that defy the boundaries of the known and the unknown.

8. THE PSYCHOLOGY OF FEAR

How Ghosts Affect the Human Mind

In the intricate dance between the seen and the unseen, the human mind grapples with a myriad of emotions, and perhaps none is as potent as fear. The question of ghosts, lurking in the shadows of our collective consciousness, taps into the primal well of dread that resides within us. In this chapter, "The Psychology of Fear," we delve into the intricate web of emotions that ghosts evoke, exploring the psychological underpinnings that shape our perception of the unseen and the chilling effect it has on the human mind.

The Evolutionary Roots of Fear

To understand the psychology of fear, we must first trace its evolutionary roots. Fear, in its most primal form, is an adaptive response that has been honed over millions of years of human evolution. The ability to sense and react to potential threats ensured the survival of our ancestors in a world teeming with predators and dangers.

In the modern context, the fear response remains deeply ingrained in our neural circuitry. When faced with a perceived threat, the brain's amygdala—the emotional centre—triggers a cascade of physiological and psychological responses. Heart rate increases, senses sharpen, and the body prepares for either fight or flight. This primal response is a testament to fear's evolutionary significance in navigating a hazardous environment.

The Uncanny Valley: Bridging the Familiar and the Strange

Ghosts, as ethereal entities that defy the laws of the natural world, often inhabit the realm of the uncanny—the unsettling space between the familiar and the unfamiliar. The concept of the uncanny, explored by Freud and later refined by robotics professor Masahiro Mori, describes the eerie feeling elicited when something closely resembles a human being but falls just short of true replication.

Ghosts, with their humanoid forms and spectral attributes, trigger the uncanny response. The brain registers them as familiar yet inherently strange, creating a cognitive dissonance that heightens our sense of unease. This phenomenon plays a pivotal role in the psychological impact of ghostly encounters, as the mind grapples with the paradoxical nature of entities that exist outside the boundaries of our everyday reality.

Cultural Conditioning and Fear

The lens through which we perceive ghosts is shaped by cultural narratives, folklore, and personal beliefs. Cultural conditioning significantly influences how individuals interpret and respond to the notion of the unseen. In cultures where ghosts are portrayed as malevolent entities seeking retribution or harboring unresolved grievances, the fear response is likely to be more pronounced.

Conversely, in cultures where ghosts are viewed as benevolent ancestors or spiritual guides, the emotional impact may be tempered by a sense of reverence or connection. The interplay between cultural conditioning and fear underscores the subjective nature of ghostly encounters, with individuals drawing on a vast tapestry of beliefs and narratives to interpret the enigmatic realm of the unseen.

The Power of Suggestion: Expectation and Experience

The human mind is susceptible to the power of suggestion, a psychological phenomenon where pre-existing beliefs and expectations influence perception. In the context of ghostly encounters, individuals who anticipate or are primed to expect a supernatural experience are more likely to interpret ambiguous stimuli as evidence of the paranormal.

This phenomenon, known as pareidolia, involves the perception of meaningful patterns, such as faces or figures, in random stimuli. In the context of ghost sightings, individuals predisposed to expect paranormal activity may interpret ordinary sounds, shadows, or reflections as manifestations of the unseen. The interplay between expectation and experience highlights the malleability of perception in the realm of the supernatural.

The Influence of Media and Popular Culture

Media, including literature, film, and television, plays a pivotal role in shaping societal perceptions of ghosts. The portrayal of ghosts in popular culture often emphasizes their eerie, malevolent, or enigmatic qualities, contributing to the cultural construction of the supernatural. Exposure to ghost stories, horror movies, and paranormal-themed content can heighten the psychological impact of the unseen by priming individuals to associate certain stimuli with ghostly phenomena.

The "primacy effect," a cognitive bias where initial information carries disproportionate weight in forming impressions, can further amplify the impact of media exposure. Individuals who are exposed to frightening depictions of ghosts may carry these impressions into real-life situations, influencing their emotional responses to ambiguous or unexplained phenomena.

Individual Differences in Fear Response

The psychology of fear is not a one-size-fits-all phenomenon. Individual differences in personality, beliefs, and prior experiences contribute to variations in the fear response to ghosts. For some, the prospect of encountering the unseen may evoke exhilaration or curiosity, while for others, it may instill paralyzing terror.

Personality traits such as openness to experience, neuroticism, and belief in the paranormal can influence how individuals approach and interpret ghostly encounters. Those with a higher tolerance for ambiguity or a predisposition toward mystical or supernatural beliefs may be more inclined to embrace the mystery of the unseen, whereas individuals with lower tolerance for uncertainty may experience heightened anxiety in the face of the unknown.

Fear as a Catalyst for Supernatural Experiences

The interplay between fear and supernatural experiences is a complex and reciprocal relationship. While fear can be a natural response to the unknown, it also has the potential to shape the very experiences that evoke it. The expectation of encountering something supernatural can elevate physiological arousal and sensory sensitivity, creating an environment conducive to the perception of paranormal phenomena.

Psychologist Michael Persinger's research on the "God helmet" experiment provides insight into the role of fear in shaping supernatural experiences. Participants exposed to weak electromagnetic fields reported sensations of a presence or a "sensed presence," highlighting the intricate connection between altered states of consciousness, environmental stimuli, and the perception of the unseen.

Post-Traumatic Stress and Hauntings

For individuals who have experienced trauma or harrowing events, the psychological impact of fear can extend into the realm of hauntings. Post-traumatic stress disorder (PTSD) can heighten vulnerability to supernatural beliefs and experiences. Traumatic memories may manifest as apparitions or ghostly phenomena, blurring the lines between psychological distress and paranormal encounters.

In cases of alleged hauntings, understanding the individual's history and psychological well-being becomes crucial. Trauma-informed approaches recognize the interconnectedness of psychological distress and paranormal experiences, emphasizing the need for sensitive and empathetic exploration of the individual's narrative.

Coping Mechanisms and Resilience

While fear of the unseen is a natural response, individuals employ various coping mechanisms to navigate the psychological challenges posed by the enigmatic realm of ghosts. Belief systems, religious or spiritual practices, and social support can serve as buffers against the psychological impact of fear. For some, the framework of organized religion provides a sense of protection and guidance, offering solace in the face of the unknown.

Cognitive reappraisal, the process of reframing and reinterpreting fearful stimuli, can also contribute to resilience in the face of ghostly encounters. Individuals who can contextualize ambiguous experiences within a rational framework may experience reduced anxiety and distress.

The Power of Rational Inquiry: Bridging the Seen and the Unseen

In navigating the haunting question of ghosts, the power of rational inquiry serves as a bridge between the seen and the unseen. Psychological frameworks, such as critical thinking and scientific scepticism, offer tools to dissect and analyze ghostly encounters within the context of naturalistic explanations.

Sceptical inquiry encourages individuals to question assumptions, evaluate evidence, and consider alternative explanations for purported supernatural phenomena. The scientific method, with its emphasis on empirical observation and testable hypotheses, provides a structured approach to investigating the unknown.

Conclusion: Unravelling the Threads of Fear and the Unseen

The psychology of fear, intertwined with the question of ghosts, illuminates the complex tapestry of human experience. From the evolutionary roots of fear to the influence of cultural narratives, individual differences, and coping mechanisms, the interplay between the seen and the unseen shapes our perceptions in profound ways.

As we navigate the enigmatic realms explored in "Glimpses of the Unseen," the psychology of fear invites us to peer into the depths of our own consciousness. The shadows that dance on the periphery of our understanding become not only a canvas for ghostly encounters but also a reflection of the intricate web of emotions that defines the human experience.

In the chapters to come, we will continue our exploration, delving into the historical dimensions, cultural perspectives, and scientific inquiries that form the rich tapestry of the haunting question of ghosts. Welcome to the ongoing journey where fear and the unseen intertwine, inviting us to unravel the threads that connect the known and the mysterious.

9.TOOLS OF THE TRADE

Technology and Methods in Ghost Hunting

Welcome to the intriguing realm of paranormal investigation, where the veil between the seen and the unseen is lifted, revealing glimpses of the mysterious and the unexplained. In this chapter, we delve into the tools of the trade that ghost hunters employ to navigate the spectral landscapes and attempt to answer the haunting question of ghosts.

The Evolution of Ghost Hunting

Ghost hunting has a rich history dating back centuries, but it wasn't until the late 19th and early 20th centuries that it began to take a more systematic and scientific approach. Today, paranormal investigators combine traditional methods with cutting-edge technology to explore the supernatural. Let's explore some of the essential tools employed in the modern ghost hunter's toolkit.

1. Electromagnetic Field (EMF) Meters

One of the fundamental concepts in paranormal investigation is the idea that ghosts or spirits may emit electromagnetic energy. EMF meters are designed to detect changes in electromagnetic fields, which are believed to be associated with paranormal activity. Investigators use these devices to measure fluctuations in electromagnetic energy levels, potentially indicating the presence of a ghostly entity.

The theory behind this is that when a spirit manifests, it may disrupt the natural electromagnetic fields in its vicinity. Ghost hunters often use EMF meters in locations where paranormal activity is suspected, such as abandoned buildings, graveyards, or historical sites.

2. Digital Voice Recorders

Capturing electronic voice phenomena (EVP) is a common goal in ghost hunting. Digital voice recorders are employed to capture audio recordings during investigations. Investigators often ask questions or make statements, hoping to receive responses from any spirits present. Upon playback, they may discover faint voices or unexplained sounds that were not audible during the investigation.

Critics argue that many EVPs can be attributed to environmental factors or audio pareidolia, where the mind perceives familiar patterns in random noise. However, proponents of EVP believe that some recordings defy explanation and offer compelling evidence of paranormal communication.

3. Thermal Imaging Cameras

Temperature fluctuations are often associated with paranormal activity. Ghost hunters use thermal imaging cameras to detect changes in temperature that may indicate the presence of a ghost. The idea is that spirits may draw on their surroundings' energy, causing temperature drops or rises.

These cameras capture infrared radiation, translating it into visible images based on temperature differences. If an investigator observes an unexplained cold spot or heat anomaly in a supposedly haunted location, it may be considered evidence of paranormal activity.

4. Spirit Boxes and Ghost Radios

Spirit boxes, or ghost radios, are devices that rapidly scan through radio frequencies, creating a continuous stream of white noise. Paranormal investigators believe that spirits can manipulate this white noise to communicate. They listen for specific words or phrases that seem to respond to their questions, suggesting a form of intelligent interaction with the unseen.

Critics argue that the random nature of radio frequency scanning can lead to auditory pareidolia, where the brain interprets random noise as meaningful. However, some investigators claim to have captured coherent and relevant responses, adding a layer of intrigue to the use of spirit boxes.

5. Motion Sensors and Trigger Objects

Motion sensors and trigger objects are employed to detect physical movement or manipulation of objects in supposedly haunted locations. Investigators may place motion sensors in areas with reported activity, hoping to capture evidence of unexplained movements. Trigger objects, on the other hand, are items deliberately placed to invite interaction from spirits. If these objects are moved or displaced without an apparent cause, investigators consider it potential evidence of paranormal activity.

6. Paranormal Apps and Software

In the age of smartphones, there's an app for everything, including ghost hunting. Numerous paranormal apps claim to detect and communicate with spirits through various means, such as EMF readings, EVP sessions, or even virtual ghost hunting experiences. While some investigators find these apps convenient and user-friendly, sceptics argue that their reliability is questionable, and they may produce false positives.

7. Psychics and Mediums

While not a technological tool, psychics and mediums play a crucial role in many paranormal investigations. These individuals claim to have heightened sensitivities or the ability to communicate with spirits directly. Investigators often collaborate with psychics to gain insights into the history of a location or to establish a connection with any spirits present.

However, the use of psychics in ghost hunting is a topic of debate within the paranormal community. Sceptics argue that psychic abilities lack scientific validation, while proponents believe that psychics can provide valuable perspectives and assistance in understanding and interpreting paranormal phenomena.

8. Scientific Measurement Tools

In addition to the more specialized tools mentioned above, ghost hunters often utilize standard scientific measurement tools to gather data during investigations. These may include digital thermometers, barometers, and even cameras equipped with full-spectrum or infrared capabilities. By collecting a variety of data, investigators aim to build a comprehensive picture of the environmental conditions during paranormal events.

Methodology in Ghost Hunting

Beyond the tools, the methodology employed by ghost hunters is a critical aspect of their investigations. It's essential to approach each case with a scientific mindset, ruling out conventional explanations before attributing occurrences to the paranormal. Here are some key principles of effective ghost hunting methodology:

1. Research and Documentation

Before conducting an investigation, thorough research into the history of the location is essential. Understanding the site's past, including any reported paranormal activity, can guide investigators in choosing the right tools and methods. Detailed documentation of the investigation process is also crucial for analysis and review.

2. Baseline Measurements

Establishing baseline measurements of environmental conditions is a crucial step. This includes recording baseline EMF levels, temperature, and other relevant data at the beginning of the investigation. Any significant deviations from these baselines during the investigation may be considered potential indicators of paranormal activity.

3. Controlled Experiments

Ghost hunters often conduct controlled experiments to test the reliability of their tools and methods. This may involve creating scenarios to provoke specific types of paranormal activity or using controlled environments to eliminate external factors that could influence the investigation.

4. Corroborating Evidence

To strengthen the validity of findings, investigators seek corroborating evidence. Multiple forms of data, such as EMF readings, EVP recordings, and visual evidence, can help build a more compelling case for paranormal activity. Corroborating evidence also involves cross-referencing historical accounts and witness testimonies.

5. Debunking and Scepticism

A crucial aspect of responsible ghost hunting is the willingness to debunk phenomena. Investigators must approach each case with a healthy dose of scepticism, actively seeking natural explanations for reported paranormal activity. By ruling out conventional causes, investigators can focus on truly unexplained occurrences.

Ethical Considerations in Ghost Hunting

While the pursuit of paranormal knowledge is exciting, ghost hunters must also be mindful of ethical considerations. Respect for the deceased, property rights, and the well-being of all involved parties should be paramount. Here are some ethical guidelines for ghost hunters to follow:

1. Obtain Permission

Before conducting an investigation, it's essential to obtain permission from property owners or authorities. Trespassing on private property or entering restricted areas without permission not only violates ethical standards but may also lead to legal consequences.

2. Respectful Conduct

Ghost hunters should conduct themselves with respect and professionalism. This includes respecting the privacy of the deceased and their families. It's crucial to avoid sensationalism and treat the investigation with the seriousness it deserves.

3. Informed Consent

When involving others in the investigation, such as witnesses, volunteers, or clients, informed consent is paramount. Clearly explain the nature of the investigation, potential risks, and the possibility of encountering unsettling phenomena. Participants should be free to withdraw from the investigation at any time.

4. Confidentiality

Investigators must respect the confidentiality of sensitive information obtained during an investigation. This includes personal stories shared by witnesses and any private details related to the location.

5. Environmental Impact

Ghost hunters should be mindful of the environmental impact of their investigations. Avoid causing damage to historical sites or natural habitats, and leave locations as they were found. Sustainable and responsible practices contribute to the preservation of both cultural and natural heritage.

The Sceptical Perspective

In the realm of ghost hunting, scepticism is a valuable tool. Sceptics argue that many reported paranormal phenomena can be explained by natural causes, psychological factors, or simple misunderstandings. It's essential to consider alternative explanations before attributing occurrences to the supernatural.

Sceptics often point out the limitations and flaws in ghost hunting tools and methodologies. They argue that subjective interpretations, cognitive biases, and the human tendency to find patterns in randomness can contribute to the perception of paranormal activity.

While sceptics may not dismiss the possibility of paranormal phenomena outright, they advocate for a rigorous scientific approach to investigations. This includes controlled experiments, peer-reviewed research, and a commitment to eliminating bias and preconceived notions.

Conclusion

Ghost hunting is a captivating journey into the unknown, blending science, technology, and a touch of the mystical. The tools of the trade, from EMF meters to digital voice recorders, offer investigators a glimpse into the elusive world of the supernatural. Yet, as technology advances and our understanding of the paranormal evolves, so too does the need for responsible and ethical ghost hunting practices.

In the pursuit of glimpses into the unseen, it's crucial to approach each investigation with a balance of scientific rigor and open-minded curiosity. Whether a skeptic, a believer, or somewhere in between, the exploration of paranormal phenomena continues to captivate the human imagination, inviting us to question the boundaries between the known and the unknowable.

10. SCEPTICS AND BELIEVERS

Debates Surrounding Ghostly Phenomena

In the realm of paranormal investigations, the clash between sceptics and believers is as old as the question of ghosts itself. As we navigate the haunting landscapes and seek glimpses of the unseen, this chapter delves into the fascinating debates and discussions that surround ghostly phenomena. From the scientific scepticism that questions the validity of every orb captured on camera to the unwavering belief in an afterlife that transcends the boundaries of the living, the clash of perspectives adds depth and complexity to the quest for understanding the supernatural.

The Sceptical Perspective

Sceptics, often rooted in the principles of scientific inquiry, approach claims of ghostly phenomena with a healthy dose of doubt. They question the reliability of evidence, the validity of eyewitness accounts, and the efficacy of the tools used in paranormal investigations. The sceptical viewpoint contends that many reported ghostly occurrences can be explained through natural and psychological factors rather than supernatural forces.

1. The Influence of Psychology

Sceptics argue that many supposed ghostly experiences can be attributed to the complexities of the human mind. Pareidolia, for instance, is a psychological phenomenon where the brain perceives familiar patterns, such as faces, in random stimuli. In the context of ghost hunting, this could lead individuals to interpret ordinary sounds or shadows as evidence of paranormal activity.

Additionally, the power of suggestion plays a significant role in shaping paranormal experiences. If individuals believe they are in a haunted location, they may interpret common occurrences, like creaking floorboards or drafts, as signs of ghostly presence. This psychological predisposition to find meaning in ambiguous stimuli can contribute to the creation of paranormal narratives.

2. Natural Explanations for Phenomena

Sceptics emphasize the importance of seeking natural explanations for reported phenomena before jumping to supernatural conclusions. For example, orbs often captured in photographs are frequently attributed to dust particles, moisture, or reflections. Sceptics argue that understanding the environmental conditions, camera settings, and potential sources of contamination is essential to demystifying these seemingly otherworldly images.

Similarly, what some interpret as cold spots indicative of ghostly presence may have more mundane explanations, such as drafts, insulation issues, or variations in environmental temperature. By exploring these natural possibilities, sceptics aim to strip away the supernatural veneer and expose the ordinary roots of seemingly extraordinary events.

3. The Limitations of Technology

While technology has become a cornerstone of paranormal investigations, sceptics question the reliability of the tools commonly used by ghost hunters. For instance, electronic voice phenomena (EVP) recordings, captured using digital voice recorders, are often criticized for their susceptibility to environmental interference and the potential for audio pareidolia.

Sceptics argue that electromagnetic field (EMF) meters, which detect changes in electromagnetic energy, may be influenced by various electronic devices and natural fluctuations. The challenge lies in differentiating between anomalous readings and those caused by everyday sources like wiring, appliances, or nearby electronic equipment.

The Believer's Perspective

On the opposite end of the spectrum are the believers, individuals who approach the question of ghosts with a deep-seated conviction in the existence of supernatural entities. Rooted in personal experiences, spiritual beliefs, or a sense of connection with the afterlife, believers find profound meaning in the unexplained and resist reductionist explanations offered by sceptics.

1. Personal Experiences and Anecdotal Evidence

Believers often point to personal experiences as the driving force behind their unwavering conviction. Ghostly encounters, inexplicable phenomena, and unexplained events shape their worldview and strengthen their belief in the existence of spirits. While sceptics may dismiss anecdotal evidence as subjective and unreliable, believers argue that these personal narratives are powerful and should not be easily dismissed.

In the absence of scientific consensus on the nature of paranormal phenomena, believers find solace and validation in shared experiences. Ghost stories passed down through generations, eyewitness accounts, and the collective wisdom of communities contribute to a rich tapestry of belief that transcends the limitations of empirical evidence.

2. Cultural and Historical Perspectives

Believers often draw on cultural and historical perspectives to support their views. Across different societies and eras, belief in spirits, ghosts, and an afterlife has been a common thread. Cultural narratives, folklore, and religious traditions offer frameworks that validate the existence of ghosts. Believers argue that the universality of these beliefs suggests a deeper, shared understanding of the supernatural.

Historical accounts of ghostly encounters, documented in literature and oral traditions, further contribute to the believer's argument. From ancient civilizations to contemporary cultures, stories of spirits interacting with the living persist, reinforcing the idea that the question of ghosts transcends time and place.

3. Spiritual and Metaphysical Perspectives

For some believers, the question of ghosts extends beyond a scientific inquiry into the nature of unexplained phenomena. Instead, it delves into the realms of spirituality and metaphysics. Many religions and spiritual practices incorporate beliefs in an afterlife, spirits, and the continuation of consciousness beyond death.

Believers often see ghostly phenomena as evidence of a connection between the material and spiritual worlds. Psychic mediums, who claim to communicate with spirits, play a crucial role in this perspective, offering a bridge between the living and the unseen. While sceptics may attribute mediumistic experiences to psychological factors, believers see them as a direct line of communication with the other side.

Finding Common Ground: The Intersection of Scepticism and Belief

While sceptics and believers may seem diametrically opposed, there is a growing recognition of the need for dialogue and understanding between these two perspectives. Bridging the gap requires an acknowledgment of the complexities inherent in the exploration of ghostly phenomena.

1. Open-minded Inquiry

Sceptics and believers alike can benefit from cultivating open-mindedness in their approach to the question of ghosts. A willingness to explore alternative viewpoints and consider new evidence, while maintaining a critical eye, can lead to a more nuanced understanding of paranormal phenomena.

2. Interdisciplinary Collaboration

Collaboration between individuals with diverse expertise—scientists, historians, psychologists, theologians, and paranormal investigators—

can enrich the study of ghostly phenomena. By bringing together different perspectives, researchers can develop more comprehensive frameworks for understanding the complex interplay of factors contributing to reported paranormal experiences.

3. Ethical Conduct in Investigations

Both sceptics and believers share a responsibility to conduct investigations ethically and responsibly. This includes respecting the privacy of individuals involved, obtaining proper permissions for investigations, and ensuring that research practices adhere to ethical standards. By upholding these principles, the field of paranormal investigation can gain credibility and foster a more inclusive dialogue.

4. Education and Public Discourse

Education plays a crucial role in fostering understanding between sceptics and believers. Public discourse, guided by accurate information and respectful dialogue, can contribute to breaking down stereotypes and dispelling misconceptions. This involves addressing the ethical considerations of paranormal investigations, the limitations of scientific methods, and the cultural diversity of belief systems.

The Grey Areas: Unanswered Questions and Unexplored Territories

As we navigate the debates between sceptics and believers, it's essential to acknowledge the grey areas—the questions that remain unanswered and the territories yet unexplored. The elusive nature of paranormal phenomena leaves room for continued inquiry and discovery. Here are some avenues for future exploration:

1. Consciousness and the Afterlife

The question of what happens to consciousness after death remains one of the most profound mysteries. Whether through scientific inquiry, philosophical exploration, or spiritual contemplation, understanding the nature of consciousness and its potential continuation beyond the physical body is a frontier that transcends the boundaries of scepticism and belief.

2. Cultural Variations in Paranormal Beliefs

Exploring the cultural variations in beliefs about ghosts can provide valuable insights into the intersection of tradition, folklore, and the human experience. Comparative studies across different societies can shed light on the ways cultural context influences the interpretation of paranormal phenomena.

3. Advancements in Technology and Parapsychology

The continuous advancements in technology offer new opportunities for investigating paranormal phenomena. Integrating the latest developments in fields such as neuroscience, parapsychology, and artificial intelligence can contribute to a more rigorous and multidisciplinary approach to the study of ghostly phenomena.

Conclusion: Navigating the Haunting Question

As we navigate the haunting question of ghosts, the debates between sceptics and believers add layers of complexity to the exploration of the unseen. The clash of perspectives, grounded in science, spirituality, or personal experience, highlights the multifaceted nature of the human response to the mysterious and the unknown.

In the journey to uncover glimpses of the unseen, perhaps the most valuable lesson lies in the recognition of shared humanity. Sceptics and believers alike are united by a common curiosity—an innate desire to understand the mysteries that linger on the periphery of our comprehension. As the debates persist, the quest for knowledge and the exploration of ghostly phenomena continue to captivate the human imagination, inviting us to venture into the shadows and seek answers to questions that transcend the boundaries of the known.

11.ETHEREAL ENTITIES

Different Types of Ghostly Appearances

I n the quest to unravel the mysteries of the supernatural, one encounters a myriad of ghostly phenomena that defy easy explanation. From translucent apparitions to shadowy figures lurking in the corners of our perception, the manifestations of ethereal entities have captivated human imagination throughout history. In this chapter, we explore the various types of ghostly appearances reported across cultures and time periods, delving into the rich tapestry of spectral encounters that contribute to the enigma of the unseen.

1. Full Apparitions: Transparent and Timeless

One of the most iconic images associated with ghosts is that of a full-bodied apparition—an ethereal figure that appears as a complete, human-like form. Witnesses often describe these entities as translucent or transparent, giving them an otherworldly quality. Full apparitions are typically reported to manifest in specific locations, often associated with traumatic events, unresolved emotions, or significant historical occurrences.

Historical Residues and Residual Hauntings

Some full apparitions are believed to be residual hauntings, wherein the ghostly figure seems to be reenacting a scene from the past. These residual energies, imprinted on the environment, play like a ghostly tapestry, revealing snippets of history to those fortunate—or perhaps unfortunate—enough to witness them. The apparitions in residual hauntings appear oblivious to their surroundings, as if trapped in a timeless loop.

Theories surrounding residual hauntings posit that intense emotions, traumatic events, or repetitive actions can leave an imprint on the fabric of space and time. This residual energy, when conditions are right, may replay like a supernatural echo, providing glimpses into moments long gone.

2. Shadow Figures: Lurking in the Periphery

In contrast to the translucent nature of full apparitions, shadow figures are characterized by their dark, often amorphous shapes. Witnesses describe these entities as shadows that move with purpose, lurking in the corners of rooms, darting through peripheral vision, or even manifesting as a dense, inky mass. The nature of shadow figures is elusive, and encounters with them often evoke a sense of foreboding.

Malevolent or Watchful Presence?

Opinions on the nature of shadow figures vary. Some believe these entities to be malevolent, feeding off fear and negative energy. Others see them as neutral observers, possibly guardians or entities that exist on a different plane of existence. The lack of distinct features in shadow figures adds to their mystery, leaving room for interpretation and speculation.

In paranormal investigations, encounters with shadow figures are often reported in locations with a history of tragedy or malevolent activities. The shadowy nature of these entities aligns with the archetype of the "shadow self" in psychology—the hidden, darker aspects of the human psyche.

3. Orbs: Mysterious Spheres of Light

Orbs are perhaps the most debated and controversial form of ghostly appearance. Typically appearing as small, spherical lights in photographs or videos, orbs are often associated with paranormal activity. However, sceptics argue that many orb sightings can be attributed to natural phenomena, such as dust particles, moisture, or lens flares.

Energy Manifestations or Contaminants?

Believers in the paranormal often interpret orbs as manifestations of spiritual energy or the presence of benevolent entities. Some paranormal investigators use orb sightings as potential indicators of ghostly activity, especially when observed in conjunction with other phenomena like EVPs or temperature fluctuations.

On the sceptical side, the argument is that the majority of orb sightings can be explained by mundane factors. Dust, pollen, and other airborne particles illuminated by camera flashes can create orb-like shapes. Understanding the environmental conditions and employing thorough analysis is essential to differentiate between potential paranormal orbs and those caused by contaminants.

4. Poltergeists: Mischievous Spirits and Physical Manifestations

The term "poltergeist" translates to "noisy ghost" in German, and these entities are known for their mischievous and often disruptive behaviour. Unlike other ghostly appearances that are primarily visual, poltergeists are associated with physical manifestations—objects moving, doors slamming, and unexplained noises.

Psychokinesis or Supernatural Entities?

The phenomenon of poltergeists is often linked to psychokinesis, the ability to influence the physical world through the mind. Some theories suggest that individuals, often unwittingly, generate this energy, leading to the seemingly paranormal activities associated with poltergeists.

However, believers in supernatural entities argue that poltergeist activity goes beyond the scope of human psychokinetic abilities. The violent and unpredictable nature of these manifestations is often difficult to reconcile with the idea of latent psychic energy.

5. Doppelgängers: Ghostly Twins and Portents of Doom

The doppelgänger, a ghostly double or look-alike of a living person, has deep roots in folklore and mythology. Encounters with one's doppelgänger are often considered ominous, with superstitions suggesting that seeing one's own double is a harbinger of tragedy or death.

Portents or Psychological Phenomena?

Psychologically, the phenomenon of seeing one's doppelgänger may be linked to altered states of consciousness, sleep paralysis, or even hallucinations. Some argue that the cultural association of doppelgängers with impending doom contributes to the fear and anxiety surrounding these apparitions.

Believers in the supernatural, however, maintain that doppelgänger sightings transcend mere psychological explanations. They suggest that these doubles may represent a form of bilocation or a momentary rift in the fabric of reality, allowing individuals to catch a glimpse of an alternate version of themselves.

6. Lady in White: Residual Spirits and Unfinished Business

The "Lady in White" is a recurring archetype in ghost lore across cultures. Often depicted as a spectral woman dressed in flowing white garments, she is associated with tragic tales of lost love, betrayal, or untimely death. Lady in White apparitions are frequently reported in locations with a history of romantic entanglements or historical tragedies.

Love, Loss, and Lingering Spirits

The stories surrounding Lady in White apparitions often involve tales of love lost, betrayal, or heartbreak. In some cases, witnesses describe the figure as appearing distressed or seeking resolution for unresolved matters. These apparitions are thought to be residual spirits caught in a loop of emotions from their past lives.

From a psychological perspective, the Lady in White may represent a cultural archetype deeply ingrained in the collective human consciousness. The enduring popularity of such apparitions in ghost stories and folklore suggests a universal fascination with themes of love, loss, and the supernatural.

7. Animal Spirits: Furred and Feathered Ghostly Companions

While the concept of ghostly apparitions is often associated with human spirits, reports of animal ghosts are not uncommon. These spectral entities may manifest as beloved pets, mythical creatures, or even wildlife associated with specific locations.

Loyal Companions Beyond the Grave

Many who have lost cherished animal companions report seeing or feeling the presence of their pets after death. These animal spirits are often described as providing comfort or reassurance, serving as loyal companions beyond the grave. Believers in the paranormal suggest that the strong emotional bonds between humans and their pets may transcend the boundary between life and death.

Sightings of mythical or legendary creatures, such as phantom black dogs or spectral horses, are also prevalent in ghost lore. These entities, often associated with folklore and regional legends, contribute to the rich tapestry of ghostly manifestations.

8. Elementals and Nature Spirits: Guardians of the Earthly Realm

In some belief systems, ethereal entities are not confined to the spirits of the deceased but extend to nature spirits and elementals. These entities are often associated with specific elements—earth, air, fire, and water—and are considered guardians or manifestations of the natural world.

Guardians of Sacred Spaces

Elementals and nature spirits are believed to inhabit sacred sites, ancient groves, or areas with significant natural energy. They are seen as protectors of the environment, and encounters with these entities are often reported by those who spend time in nature or explore mystical landscapes.

While the existence of elementals and nature spirits is rooted in spiritual and esoteric traditions, encounters with these entities may also be interpreted through the lens of ecological consciousness and the deep connection between humans and the natural world.

9. Time Slips and Residual Time Distortions

Beyond traditional ghostly appearances, some witnesses report experiencing time slips or residual time distortions. These phenomena involve brief moments where individuals perceive events or scenes from the past or future, seemingly crossing temporal boundaries.

Temporal Anomalies and Haunting Echoes

Time slips are often associated with specific locations, where the fabric of time appears to be thin or distorted. Witnesses may suddenly find themselves in a different era, witnessing scenes or interacting with entities from the past or future. These temporal anomalies add a layer of complexity to the exploration of ghostly phenomena, challenging our understanding of time and reality.

Theories surrounding time slips range from the influence of electromagnetic fields to the existence of parallel dimensions. These encounters, while rare, contribute to the overarching question of the nature of time and its potential fluidity.

Conclusion: Unravelling the Tapestry of the Unseen

As we navigate the haunting question of ghosts, the diverse manifestations of ethereal entities paint a complex picture of the supernatural. From full-bodied apparitions to shadowy figures and time slips, the various types of ghostly appearances contribute to the rich tapestry of the unseen.

While sceptics may seek scientific explanations for these phenomena, believers find validation in personal experiences, cultural traditions, and spiritual beliefs. The debates surrounding ghostly appearances continue to captivate the human imagination, inviting us to explore the boundaries between the known and the unknown.

In the journey to unravel the mysteries of ethereal entities, perhaps the most profound realization is that the question of ghosts transcends mere classification. It beckons us to consider the interconnectedness of human consciousness, the enduring power of folklore, and the boundless possibilities inherent in the exploration of the supernatural.

As we navigate the haunting landscapes, we are reminded that the unseen, with all its enigmatic facets, continues to inspire wonder, curiosity, and a deep reverence for the mysteries that linger just beyond the edge of perception.

12.BEYOND THE GRAVE

Communication with the Spirit World

I n the pursuit of understanding the mysteries that lie beyond our immediate perception, one of the most compelling aspects of paranormal investigation is the attempt to communicate with the spirit world. Whether driven by a desire to connect with departed loved ones, seek guidance from ethereal entities, or unravel the enigma of life after death, the exploration of communication beyond the grave is a central theme in the tapestry of the unseen. In this chapter, we delve into the methods, experiences, and implications of attempting to bridge the gap between the living and the spirit world.

1. Mediumship: Bridges Between Realms

At the heart of communication with the spirit world is the practice of mediumship. Mediums, individuals who claim the ability to act as intermediaries between the living and the deceased, have played a central role in spiritual and metaphysical traditions throughout history.

Types of Mediumship

Mediumship takes various forms, each with its own methods and purported abilities.

- **Physical Mediumship:** Involves tangible, observable phenomena, such as levitation of objects, materialization of spirits, or even direct communication through physical manifestations. Séances, where a group of individuals gathers to communicate with spirits, often involve physical mediumship.

- **Mental Mediumship:** Focuses on communication through the medium's mind. This can include receiving messages, impressions, or visions from spirits, which are then relayed to those seeking contact. Mental mediums may also practice automatic writing, allowing the spirits to influence their written words.
- **Trance Mediumship:** Involves the medium entering an altered state of consciousness, allowing a spirit entity to communicate directly through them. The medium may speak, write, or convey messages while in this trance state.

Challenges and Scepticism

While many individuals attest to profound experiences with mediums, scepticism surrounds the practice. Critics argue that mediums may use cold reading techniques, where they make general statements that could apply to many individuals, or hot reading, where they gather information about participants in advance. The challenge lies in distinguishing genuine mediumistic abilities from the potential for deception or self-deception.

2. EVP (Electronic Voice Phenomena): Voices from Beyond

In the age of technology, electronic devices have become tools for attempting to capture direct communication from the spirit world. Electronic Voice Phenomena (EVP) refers to the purported voices or sounds of spirits captured on audio recordings.

Recording Sessions and Interpretation

Paranormal investigators often conduct EVP sessions in locations with reported ghostly activity. They use digital voice recorders to capture ambient sounds while posing questions to any potential spirits present. During playback, investigators listen for unexplained voices or responses that were not audible during the recording.

Interpreting EVP can be subjective, as what one person hears may differ from another's interpretation. Believers argue that some EVPs contain clear and relevant responses to specific questions, providing evidence of communication with spirits. Sceptics, on the other hand, attribute EVPs to environmental noise, radio interference, or the tendency of the human mind to find patterns in random sounds.

3. Spirit Boards and Divination Tools

Spirit boards, popularly known as Ouija boards, have been used for centuries as tools to communicate with the spirit world. These boards feature letters, numbers, and other symbols, and participants place their hands on a planchette that moves to spell out messages.

The Ideomotor Effect and Subconscious Influence

The ideomotor effect, where subconscious or involuntary muscle movements influence the motion of the planchette, is often cited as a natural explanation for Ouija board movements. Sceptics argue that participants may unknowingly guide the planchette based on their expectations or collective thoughts.

However, believers in the paranormal see Ouija boards as powerful divination tools that can facilitate direct communication with spirits. The experiences reported by users range from seemingly random movements to detailed and coherent messages.

4. Psychics and Clairvoyants: Insights Beyond the Veil

Psychics and clairvoyants claim to possess heightened sensitivities or extrasensory perceptions that allow them to perceive information beyond the scope of the ordinary senses. These individuals may receive messages, visions, or impressions from spirits, offering insights into the past, present, or future.

Remote Viewing and Psychic Impressions

Some psychics practice remote viewing, where they claim to see or sense events or locations beyond their immediate physical surroundings. Psychic impressions can take various forms, from symbolic visions to emotional sensations related to the spirits they encounter.

Critics often attribute psychic experiences to intuition, psychology, or the power of suggestion. However, proponents argue that genuine psychic abilities provide valuable insights and connections to the spirit world.

5. Dream Visitation: Nightly Encounters with the Departed

Dreams have long been considered a realm where the boundaries between the living and the deceased may blur. Many individuals report dreams that involve communication with departed loved ones, offering comfort, guidance, or closure.

Symbolism and Personal Significance

Dreams involving the deceased are often highly symbolic and open to interpretation. While sceptics attribute such experiences to the workings of the subconscious mind, believers find profound meaning in dream visitations. The departed may convey messages through symbols, emotions, or even direct conversations in the dream realm.

6. Personal Items and Object Linking: Ties to the Past

Object linking involves using personal items or belongings to establish a connection with the spirit world. This practice relies on the belief that objects can retain energy or memories associated with their owners, allowing for a potential link between the living and the departed.

Psychometry and Energetic Residue

Psychometry, a related practice, involves obtaining information about a person or event by touching an object associated with it. Practitioners claim to receive impressions, visions, or emotions related to the object's history.

While sceptics attribute these experiences to the power of suggestion, believers argue that personal items can carry energetic residue from their owners, providing a tangible link to the spirit world.

7. Near-Death Experiences (NDEs): Brief Journeys Beyond Life

Near-death experiences occur when individuals, often in life-threatening situations, report leaving their bodies and entering a realm beyond the physical. These profound encounters may include encounters with deceased loved ones, a review of one's life, or a sense of moving towards a light.

Spiritual Transcendence and Afterlife Glimpses

Near-death experiences often describe a sense of peace, love, and acceptance in the presence of departed friends or family members. While some sceptics argue that these experiences result from physiological processes in the brain, believers see NDEs as glimpses into the afterlife.

The consistent themes in near-death experiences, regardless of cultural or religious background, contribute to the ongoing dialogue about the nature of consciousness and the possibility of life after death.

8. Oracular Practices and Divination: Seeking Guidance from Beyond

Throughout history, various cultures have engaged in oracular practices to seek guidance or communicate with the spirit world. Oracles, diviners, and shamans employ rituals, symbols, or altered states of consciousness to access insights beyond ordinary perception.

The Delphic Oracle and Ancient Traditions

In ancient Greece, the Delphic Oracle was renowned for providing prophetic guidance. Similar practices were prevalent in cultures around the world, where individuals with a purported connection to the spirit world offered insights and predictions.

While oracular practices are often steeped in cultural and religious traditions, their relevance endures in modern metaphysical and spiritual communities.

9. Scientific Perspectives: Exploring the Unseen with Technology

In recent years, advancements in technology have provided new avenues for exploring the mysteries of the unseen. Researchers and inventors are developing tools and devices aimed at detecting and communicating with spirits through scientific means.

Ghost Hunting Equipment and Sensor Technologies

Ghost hunters often employ a range of equipment, including electromagnetic field (EMF) meters, thermal cameras, and motion sensors, to detect anomalies associated with paranormal activity. These tools are used in conjunction with traditional methods to gather data and evidence during investigations.

The challenge lies in interpreting the data collected and distinguishing between natural environmental factors and potential spirit-related phenomena. Sceptics argue that much of the evidence gathered through ghost hunting equipment can be explained by mundane factors.

Conclusion: Navigating the Threshold

As we navigate the threshold between the living and the spirit world, the methods and experiences of communication beyond the grave remain a subject of profound fascination, debate, and contemplation. Whether through the age-old practices of mediumship, the use of modern technology, or the exploration of dreams and altered states of consciousness, humanity continues to seek connection and understanding with the unseen.

Sceptics and believers alike contribute to the ongoing dialogue about the nature of consciousness, the afterlife, and the potential for communication with entities beyond our immediate understanding. The diverse approaches to bridging the gap between realms offer a rich tapestry of perspectives, inviting us to question, explore, and contemplate the mysteries that linger just beyond the edge of perception.

In the pursuit of glimpses into the unseen, it is crucial to approach these experiences with a balance of open-minded curiosity and critical inquiry. The exploration of communication beyond the grave, with all its complexities and nuances, continues to captivate the human imagination, inviting us to venture into the realms of the unknown and seek answers to questions that transcend the boundaries of the material world.

13. GHOSTS IN POPULAR CULTURE

From Literature to Film

In the vast tapestry of human storytelling, ghosts have long been prominent figures, haunting the pages of literature and flickering on the silver screen. As we navigate the haunting question of ghosts, it is essential to explore the profound impact these spectral entities have had on popular culture. This chapter delves into the rich history of ghosts in literature and film, tracing their evolution from ancient folklore to contemporary tales that continue to captivate audiences worldwide.

The Ghostly Muse: Literature's Enduring Spirits

Ancient Roots and Folklore

Ghosts have deep roots in the folklore of cultures around the world. From the vengeful spirits of ancient Greece to the spectral apparitions of Chinese folklore, the idea of entities lingering beyond death has permeated human storytelling for centuries. These tales often served dual purposes: to caution against moral transgressions and to offer a narrative thread connecting the living with the realm of the unseen.

Gothic Literature and Romantic Ghosts

The 18th and 19th centuries witnessed a surge of interest in the macabre and supernatural, giving rise to Gothic literature. Writers like Edgar Allan Poe, Mary Shelley, and the Brontë sisters wove tales of haunted castles, tormented spirits, and undying love that transcended the grave. Ghosts in Gothic literature became metaphors for repressed desires, societal anxieties, and the unresolved conflicts that linger in the human psyche.

Victorian Spiritualism and Ghostly Communication

The Victorian era saw a resurgence of interest in spiritualism, a movement that sought to communicate with the spirit world. Séances, mediums, and Ouija boards became popular avenues for attempting to bridge the gap between the living and the dead. This fascination with spiritual communication left an indelible mark on literature, with ghostly themes permeating works like Charles Dickens' "A Christmas Carol" and Henry James' "The Turn of the Screw."

Modern Hauntings: From M.R. James to Shirley Jackson

The early 20th century brought a shift in ghost storytelling. Authors like M.R. James and Algernon Blackwood introduced a more psychological and subtle approach to the supernatural. Shirley Jackson's "The Haunting of Hill House" (1959) further explored the intricacies of haunted minds, laying the groundwork for psychological horror that would become a staple in ghost literature.

Cinematic Spectres: Ghosts on the Silver Screen

Silent Beginnings: "The Cabinet of Dr. Caligari" (1920)

The silent film era introduced audiences to the visual language of ghosts and the supernatural. German Expressionist cinema, exemplified by films like "The Cabinet of Dr. Caligari," employed distorted sets and eerie visuals to create an unsettling atmosphere. While not explicitly about ghosts, these films set the stage for the spectral aesthetics that would later define the horror genre.

Classic Hollywood Horrors: "Topper" (1937) and "The Uninvited" (1944)

As Hollywood embraced the horror genre, ghosts took on various roles, from comedic to terrifying. "Topper" (1937), a screwball comedy about a man haunted by two playful ghosts, offered a light-hearted take on spectral encounters. Contrastingly, "The Uninvited" (1944) explored the darker side of haunting, blending romance with supernatural horror and paving the way for ghostly narratives in film noir.

The Golden Age of Japanese Horror: "Kwaidan" (1964) and "Ringu" (1998)

Japanese cinema has a rich tradition of ghost stories, known as "kaidan." Films like "Kwaidan" (1964), an anthology of supernatural tales, and "Ringu" (1998), which spawned an international wave of J-horror, demonstrated the cultural nuances and psychological depth that Japanese ghost stories bring to the cinematic landscape.

The Ghostly Renaissance: "The Others" (2001) and "The Sixth Sense" (1999)

The turn of the 21st century marked a resurgence of interest in ghostly narratives, with films like "The Sixth Sense" and "The Others" redefining the genre. These films combined atmospheric storytelling with unexpected twists, challenging audiences to reconsider their perceptions of the supernatural.

Contemporary Horrors: "The Conjuring" Universe and "Hereditary" (2018)

In recent years, the horror genre has experienced a renaissance, with ghosts and hauntings taking centre stage. "The Conjuring" universe, anchored by Ed and Lorraine Warren's paranormal investigations, and "Hereditary," a family drama entwined with supernatural elements, exemplify the genre's ability to evolve and blend with other storytelling motifs.

Television's Haunting Tales: From Anthologies to Supernatural Epics

The Twilight Zone: A Dimension of Ghostly Imagination

"The Twilight Zone," created by Rod Serling, brought a new dimension to television storytelling. This anthology series explored the eerie, the mysterious, and the supernatural, often featuring episodes with ghostly twists and moral allegories. From the iconic "Nightmare at 20,000

Feet" to the thought-provoking "The Hitch-Hiker," the series left an indelible mark on the portrayal of ghosts on television.

Haunted Mansions and Eccentric Detectives: The Ghosts of Scooby-Doo

Children and adults alike have encountered ghosts through the adventures of Scooby-Doo and the Mystery Inc. gang. While primarily a comedic exploration of the supernatural, the series has contributed to shaping perceptions of ghosts for generations, combining spooky mysteries with humor and camaraderie.

Supernatural Epics: "Buffy the Vampire Slayer" (1997-2003) and "The Haunting of Hill House" (2018)

Television has evolved to embrace long-form storytelling, allowing for in-depth exploration of ghostly themes. "Buffy the Vampire Slayer" seamlessly integrated supernatural elements with the struggles of adolescence, while "The Haunting of Hill House" redefined the haunted house narrative by combining family drama with chilling horror.

Video Games: Interactive Ghostly Encounters

The rise of video games as a storytelling medium has ushered in a new era of interactive ghostly encounters. Games like "Fatal Frame," "Silent Hill," and "Phasmophobia" allow players to step into the shoes of characters facing spectral entities, blurring the line between audience and protagonist.

Immersive Horror: "PT" (2014) and Virtual Reality Experiences

In the realm of virtual reality, horror experiences like "PT" (Playable Teaser) have pushed the boundaries of immersive storytelling. These experiences offer players a first-person perspective, intensifying the psychological impact of ghostly encounters and elevating horror to new heights.

The Evolution of Ghost Stories: A Reflection of Society

Changing Representations: From Malevolence to Sympathy

The portrayal of ghosts in popular culture has evolved from malevolent entities seeking revenge to more sympathetic figures with unresolved issues. This shift reflects changing societal attitudes toward death, grief, and the afterlife, offering nuanced perspectives on the complexities of the human experience.

Meta-Narratives and Self-Reflective Ghost Stories

Recent ghost stories often incorporate meta-narratives, exploring the act of storytelling itself. Films like "Crimson Peak" (2015) and "The Babadook" (2014) use ghosts as metaphors for trauma and repressed emotions, inviting audiences to engage with narratives that transcend traditional horror conventions.

Conclusion: Haunting Echoes in the Collective Imagination

As we navigate the haunting question of ghosts, the realms of literature, film, television, and video games offer a kaleidoscopic view of spectral encounters. From ancient folklore to modern storytelling, ghosts have woven themselves into the fabric of our collective imagination, transcending cultural boundaries and evolving to reflect the complexities of the human psyche.

Ghosts in popular culture are not merely entities that go bump in the night; they are reflections of our fears, desires, and the lingering questions that define our existence. As technology advances and storytelling methods continue to evolve, one thing remains constant—the timeless allure of the unseen, inviting us to peer into the shadows and catch glimpses of the spectral echoes that resonate across the ages.

14.HAUNTED HISTORIES

Uncovering the Past through Ghostly Lens

In the exploration of the unseen, the connection between ghosts and history is a profound and intricate tapestry. Ghostly apparitions, whether residual echoes of the past or entities with unresolved business, often become intertwined with the historical narratives of the places they haunt. This chapter delves into the fascinating intersection of ghosts and history, exploring how spectral encounters offer glimpses into bygone eras and the untold stories that linger in the shadows.

1. Residual Hauntings: Echoes of the Past

The Imprint of History

Residual hauntings, a phenomenon where ghostly apparitions seem to replay past events like a spectral tapestry, provide a unique lens through which to view history. Locations with deep historical significance, such as battlefields, castles, and old mansions, often bear the imprints of the intense emotions and traumatic events that unfolded within their walls.

Civil War Battlefields: Ghosts of Conflict

In the United States, Civil War battlefields stand as poignant reminders of a nation divided. Reports of residual hauntings in places like Gettysburg and Antietam suggest that the echoes of gunfire, the cries of soldiers, and the anguish of lives lost may persist in the collective memory of these landscapes.

The Tower of London: A Tapestry of Suffering

The Tower of London, with its rich and often grisly history, is reputed to be one of the most haunted places in the world. Residual hauntings within its walls evoke the spectre of historical figures like Anne Boleyn and Thomas More, offering glimpses into the turbulent times of Tudor England.

2. Intelligent Hauntings: Conversations Across Time

Historical Figures and Ghostly Encounters

Intelligent hauntings, where entities demonstrate awareness and interact with the living, open a door to conversations across time. Reports of encounters with historical figures, whether in grand palaces or humble cottages, provide a unique perspective on the lives and personalities of those who shaped the course of history.

The Ghosts of Presidents: White House Chronicles

The White House, the iconic residence of U.S. presidents, is said to be inhabited not only by the living but also by the spectral remnants of past leaders. From Abraham Lincoln's apparition, often associated with pivotal moments in national history, to sightings of First Ladies and other prominent figures, the ghosts of the White House weave a tapestry of political and personal histories.

Royal Residencies: England's Ghostly Monarchs

In England, the castles and palaces that once housed monarchs bear witness to centuries of political intrigue, wars, and personal dramas. Windsor Castle, Hampton Court Palace, and the Tower of London are among the locations where reports of ghostly apparitions contribute to the living history of the British monarchy.

3. Architectural Ghosts: Spirits in Stone and Wood

Historic Buildings and Ghostly Guardians

Architectural marvels from different eras often carry the weight of history within their walls. Reports of ghostly manifestations in ancient cathedrals, medieval castles, and colonial mansions provide a unique lens through which to appreciate the craftsmanship and historical significance of these structures.

Colonial Williamsburg: An Ephemeral Glimpse into America's Past

Colonial Williamsburg, a meticulously restored living history museum, is not only a testament to preservation but also a site of reported ghostly encounters. Visitors describe interactions with apparitions in period clothing, offering an ephemeral glimpse into the daily lives and struggles of those who lived during the American colonial period.

The Ancient City of Pompeii: Echoes of Catastrophe

The ruins of Pompeii, frozen in time by the eruption of Mount Vesuvius in 79 AD, bear witness to a tragically abrupt end. Reports of ghostly encounters in the archaeological site suggest that the imprints of daily life, sudden panic, and untimely death may linger in the ancient streets and buildings.

4. Historical Trauma and Ghostly Resonance

Dark Chapters and Lingering Spirits

Some places carry the weight of historical trauma, and the ghosts associated with such locations often reflect the anguish and suffering of the past. From former slave plantations to concentration camps, these sites become haunted not only by the events that transpired but also by the souls who endured unthinkable hardships.

Alcatraz Island: The Haunting Legacy of a Penitentiary

Alcatraz, the infamous island prison in San Francisco Bay, witnessed decades of incarceration and hardship. Reports of ghostly apparitions, echoing the despair of inmates and the brutality of the environment, contribute to the haunting legacy of Alcatraz and its place in American history.

Hiroshima and Nagasaki: Spirits of the Atomic Past

The atomic bombings of Hiroshima and Nagasaki in 1945 left an indelible mark on history. Reports of ghostly encounters in the aftermath of these tragic events suggest a lingering resonance, a connection between the living and the departed that transcends the boundaries of time and space.

5. Unearthing Hidden Histories: Archaeology and the Supernatural

Buried Secrets and Unseen Presences

Archaeological excavations often uncover hidden histories, but they can also reveal the presence of the unseen. Reports of ghostly encounters during archaeological digs, whether in ancient burial grounds or forgotten ruins, add an extra layer of complexity to the exploration of human history.

The Screaming Skulls of England: Supernatural Sentinels

Legend has it that certain skulls, often discovered during renovations or excavations, are bound to the places they once inhabited. The stories of the Screaming Skulls of England, each associated with a specific location and a tragic tale, add an eerie dimension to the intersection of archaeology and the supernatural.

6. Paranormal Investigations: Bridging History and the Unseen

Tools of the Trade: Technology and Methodology

Paranormal investigators, armed with an array of tools and methodologies, seek to bridge the gap between history and the unseen. From electromagnetic field (EMF) meters to infrared cameras, these tools are used to detect anomalies and gather evidence of ghostly activity in historical locations.

The Stanley Hotel: A Portal to the Past

The Stanley Hotel in Colorado, known for inspiring Stephen King's "The Shining," has become a focal point for paranormal investigations. Ghost hunters and enthusiasts explore the hotel's historic corridors, attempting to capture evidence of spectral encounters and gain insights into the mysteries that may linger within its walls.

Conclusion: Echoes of Ages Past

As we navigate the haunting question of ghosts, the intertwining of spectral encounters with historical narratives creates a profound and intricate tapestry. Whether through residual hauntings that echo the events of bygone eras, intelligent hauntings that offer conversations across time, or the architectural ghosts that inhabit historic structures, ghosts become custodians of untold stories and unseen perspectives.

Haunted histories remind us that the past is not a static entity confined to textbooks and archives; it is a living, breathing force that resonates in the present. The ghosts that linger in historical sites and hidden corners invite us to explore, reflect, and uncover the layers of human experience that transcend the boundaries of time. In the dance between history and the unseen, we find echoes of ages past, weaving a narrative that transcends the limits of the tangible and beckons us to gaze into the shadows of our shared heritage.

15. THE FUTURE OF GHOST STUDIES

Emerging Trends and Unanswered Questions

In the ever-evolving landscape of paranormal investigation and ghost studies, the future holds both the promise of new discoveries and the challenge of unravelling age-old mysteries. As we navigate the haunting question of ghosts, this chapter explores the emerging trends and unanswered questions that define the forefront of ghost studies. From advancements in technology to the philosophical implications of the unseen, we delve into the evolving nature of our quest to understand the paranormal.

1. Advancements in Technology: Ghost Hunting in the Digital Age

The Rise of Augmented Reality (AR) and Virtual Reality (VR)

As technology continues to advance, augmented reality (AR) and virtual reality (VR) are poised to revolutionize the way we perceive and interact with the paranormal. Imagine a future where investigators can use AR glasses to overlay historical scenes onto present-day landscapes, providing a glimpse into the past and potentially revealing lingering spirits tied to historical events.

Virtual reality, with its immersive capabilities, may allow researchers to create controlled environments for paranormal experiments, offering a more controlled and repeatable approach to studying ghostly phenomena. This technology could also enable individuals to explore haunted locations from the comfort of their homes, democratizing access to the paranormal.

Quantum Computing and Anomalies in Spacetime

The intersection of quantum computing and paranormal studies opens up intriguing possibilities. Quantum computers, with their ability to process vast amounts of data simultaneously, could enhance our understanding of anomalies in spacetime associated with ghostly encounters. Exploring the quantum nature of consciousness and its potential connection to the afterlife remains a tantalizing avenue for future research.

2. Psychology and Consciousness: Probing the Depths of Human Experience

Neuroscientific Approaches to Paranormal Experiences

Advancements in neuroscience offer an unprecedented opportunity to explore the brain's role in paranormal encounters. Researchers may delve into the neural mechanisms underlying apparitions, auditory phenomena, and altered states of consciousness associated with ghostly experiences. Understanding the neurobiology of belief and perception could provide valuable insights into the nature of ghost sightings and encounters.

Consciousness Studies and Interconnected Realities

The exploration of consciousness and its relationship to the paranormal opens up philosophical and metaphysical inquiries. Researchers may delve into theories suggesting that consciousness extends beyond individual minds, connecting individuals to broader, unseen realms. Exploring the interconnected nature of consciousness could reshape our understanding of the afterlife and the potential for communication with entities beyond the physical realm.

3. Cross-Cultural Perspectives: Global Insights into the Unseen

Comparative Folklore and Ghost Archetypes

Cross-cultural studies in folklore and mythology offer a rich tapestry of ghostly archetypes and narratives. Future research may focus on identifying common themes and motifs in ghost stories from different cultures, shedding light on universal human experiences and fears. Comparative folklore studies could contribute to a deeper understanding of the psychological and cultural roots of ghost beliefs.

Global Collaborations in Paranormal Research

The future of ghost studies may involve increased collaboration among researchers from diverse cultural backgrounds. Global perspectives and collaborative investigations could lead to a more comprehensive understanding of paranormal phenomena. By combining indigenous knowledge, traditional beliefs, and modern research methodologies, scholars may uncover new dimensions of the unseen that transcend cultural boundaries.

4. Ethics and Respect in Paranormal Investigations

Ethical Considerations in Ghost Hunting

As paranormal investigations gain mainstream attention, the ethical dimensions of ghost hunting come into focus. Researchers and investigators may grapple with questions of consent, privacy, and the potential impact of their activities on both the living and the unseen. Establishing ethical guidelines and practices within the field becomes essential to ensure responsible and respectful engagement with the paranormal.

Community Involvement and Local Perspectives

Future ghost studies may increasingly involve collaboration with local communities and individuals who have first-hand experiences with the paranormal. Engaging with the perspectives of those living in haunted locales can provide valuable insights, foster understanding, and contribute to the preservation of cultural heritage associated with ghostly legends.

5. Quantifiable Evidence and Sceptical Inquiry

Standardized Protocols for Paranormal Investigations

The establishment of standardized protocols for paranormal investigations is an ongoing trend in the field. As ghost studies move toward greater scientific rigor, researchers may adopt systematic methodologies and measurement tools to collect quantifiable data. This shift aims to enhance the credibility of paranormal research and facilitate collaboration with mainstream scientific disciplines.

Sceptical Inquiry and the Scientific Method

Scepticism remains a crucial element in the pursuit of understanding the paranormal. Embracing the scientific method and encouraging critical thinking within the field of ghost studies can help differentiate between genuine phenomena and misinterpretations. Sceptical inquiry contributes to the refinement of research methodologies and ensures a balanced approach to investigating the unseen.

6. Public Engagement and Education: Bridging the Gap

Public Awareness and Destigmatization

With the rise of paranormal-themed television shows and podcasts, public interest in ghost studies has surged. Future trends may involve initiatives to educate the public about the scientific aspects of paranormal research, destigmatize discussions about the unseen, and promote responsible engagement with the paranormal. Bridging the gap between researchers and the public can foster a more informed and respectful discourse.

Paranormal Education and Academic Integration

The integration of paranormal studies into academic curricula represents a potential future trend. Establishing courses or academic programs dedicated to the scientific study of the paranormal could provide a structured framework for aspiring researchers and investigators. Academic recognition can contribute to the legitimacy and institutionalization of ghost studies.

Conclusion: Navigating the Unseen Frontiers

As we navigate the haunting question of ghosts, the future of ghost studies holds the promise of a multidisciplinary and globally informed exploration of the paranormal. From technological advancements to ethical considerations, the evolving nature of our quest to understand the unseen invites researchers, sceptics, and enthusiasts alike to embark on a journey that transcends the boundaries of conventional knowledge.

The unanswered questions that linger in the shadows of ghost studies beckon us to venture into uncharted territories, armed with curiosity, respect, and a commitment to unravelling the mysteries that have captivated human imagination for centuries. The future promises not only glimpses of the unseen but also a deeper understanding of the interconnected threads that weave through the fabric of our existence.

Milton Keynes UK
Ingram Content Group UK Ltd.
UKHW051916011223
433620UK00011B/493